Facebook Advertising

The Beginner's Guide for Facebook Marketing: How to Turn Your Facebook Audience into Real-time Sales, the Best Strategies Used to Make Effective and Efficient Facebook Ads.

MICHAEL ROBERT FORTUNATE

TABLE OF CONTENTS

INTRODUCTION

Congratulations on purchasing *Facebook Advertising*: *The Beginner's Guide for Facebook Marketing*. We live in a digital era where social media influence in our daily lives cannot be underestimated. Several billion people are present on digital platforms on a daily basis. Facebook makes one of the most popular social media platforms in this era. New and established businesses are moving in the digital direction and growing significantly from being on social media platforms. Facebook has audiences from all over the world to satisfy different businesses in various industries.

Serious entrepreneurs understand how crucial it is to advertise their businesses and products on Facebook. An estimated 80% of all the users of the internet are on Facebook. Over 60% of adults around the world use Facebook. This translates to billions of audiences that will be exposed to an advert when posted.

Facebook advertising suits businesses in all levels of entrepreneurship, whether you are a startup or an established business or brand; a Facebook platform will ultimately increase your sales significantly. The costs of Facebook advertising are seemingly low compared to conventional methods of advertising. In addition, you can be guaranteed to reap handsomely from Facebook advertising. There is no much time wastage with Facebook advertising as it is fast and efficient.

From the information above, you can already tell that there is indeed a great need to advertise on Facebook. The questions that may linger on your minds are:

1. How to start Facebook advertising?

2. How to make Facebook advertising work for your business?

3. How to attract the kind of audience you need on Facebook?

These and other specifics of social media marketing on Facebook are detailed here. The book will open your eyes to the world of digital marketing, specifically on Facebook and how to use it to your advantage. There are plenty of books on this subject on the market, thanks again for choosing this one! Every effort was made to ensure it is full of as much useful information as possible; please enjoy!

CHAPTER 1: CONVERTING FACEBOOK ADS TO REAL-TIME SALES

Facebook has a relatively higher number of users than any other social media platforms. It, therefore, allows every business to interact with many potential clients. When many people see your products, it increases the chance of getting many buyers. However, traffic is not everything any seller wants for the business. It is more fulfilling when a business person achieves sales from Facebook traffic. The dream of every business person is to get a good number of sales after they put up an advertisement. Sadly, this is not always the case. Some Ads do not even get noticed, and if they do, they do not get any clicks. When a seller realizes that even with the traffic, they don't get clicks, it sends a signal that probably something is not right with the Ad. It's human nature to want to know more about anything attractive that comes their way.

To have more people notice and get eager to know more about your product, let us look at some tips and tricks to consider when creating your Ads.

Get Catchy Images to Use for The Ads

The first image has to stand out more than anything else to ensure everybody will see it as they scroll down their Facebook account. High-quality images are most suitable for this purpose. Images should be bright and full of color to make them easily noticeable. When they include photos of people, they should show happy people to win the Ad more clicks. The images will do even better if they feature the people using your products. At the same time, it's essential to consider the target population. A photo of a happy attractive lady will cause more men to click on the Ad and vice versa. For general products where the community gender doesn't matter, photos of beautiful ladies will do well in catching the attention of both genders.

It's advisable to use personal images so that the actual product corresponds with the Ad. Professional photography is on the rise has made it easier for sellers to get quality photographs of their products. However, a few sellers might not afford professional photos due to the attached cost. In this case, an excellent mobile phone or camera comes in handy and can be used to get outstanding images. Here are some tips to get beautiful photos without professional help;

- Keep the background clear so that the product stands out well;
- Ensure the product is clean and in its best state;
- Ensure you have good lighting so that the photos will give a view of the real product. Poor lighting also affects the color which may cause problems with some customers;
- Get several pictures from different angles to capture all the essential product details. For instance, someone selling a car will capture the outside and the interior, considering the most crucial information.

Include Important Product Details

Every product has featured that customers want to know. If it's a new product in the market, indicating details will make people understand it and probably get interested in having it. Ensure that you give details that are of interest before they ask. Some may not even ask because they don't get to think about it. Do your research to know what features most people will most likely get interested in knowing. Use those details for your product description. For instance, if you are selling shoes, most people will want a seller to indicate the material used, sizes, and colors available as well as the gender they suit. Therefore, a description of a shoe would look like;

'Unisex canvas shoes with a rubber sole,

Available in blue, black and white colors

Sizes 38 – 44

Delivery is done within 12 hours after confirming the order.'

Some viewers will get interested in the product after they have seen its details. Like any young person will get interested in a mobile phone that features an excellent camera. The person does not just view the Ad because he needs a mobile phone but because the features indicated are attractive to him. Other people will look for an Ad that gives the details on the spot because they don't want to contact many sellers. For example, someone will search, *'white canvas shoes'* because they want to narrow down their search to just what they want. A list of Ads with the three words will show at the top of the list. If a seller with the same shoes only indicated *'shoes for sale,'* the advert might come at the end of the list, and the client may not scroll to the bottom. Details will also make it easier for the seller to reduce the number of similar questions he receives. Some people are not patient enough to wait for a response if it's not instant. By giving all the necessary details, you can keep serious buyers in your 'shop' and get time to respond to them effectively.

Indicate Product Price Clearly

Once someone gets interested in a product, the next thing they want to know is the price. If the seller considers indicating the last amount on his Ad, it is good for him to specify that his price is fixed. This detail will help to avoid many messages of people who want to negotiate. However, it's advisable that you price your products higher, to give an allowance for negotiation. It's in many people's likings to negotiate for discounts, therefore, having a provision for the 'make offer' button adds to the number of people who contact you. Once a potential buyer contacts a seller, it's evident that they have considered buying the product and it's easier to convince them to buy at that point. Do enough research and know your competitors' prices. This knowledge will help you ensure that you don't set your prices too low or too high, lest you put off potential buyers.

Make the Company Policies Clear

Every company, big or small, should have well-laid policies. These will help the people who view their profile understand the company operations even before they engage. It also gives the buyers confidence because they feel that they are dealing with a serious seller who is well established. It makes it easier to convince such clients to buy since they know that the company is respectable. After the first successful purchase, most of the buyers will want to come back or refer their loved ones due to the trust they already have in you.

Company policies also help handle the expectations of potential buyers. This is because when they engage the seller, they already have an idea of what they expect and won't expect otherwise.

Create Separate Ads for Different Products

A seller can be tempted to put all his items in one ad, but it's not advisable to have them all together. It's good to have different Ads for different things. This way, all items will have equal chances, as different people may want to view different products. The best strategy to capture potential clients is through images, and people will rarely scroll through Ads to look for what they want if it's not in the displayed image.

In case you have a general sale, you can indicate it at the bottom of the Ad, and interested people will scroll through your wall to view the other products. You can also attach a link that directs buyers to your wall. This way, clients who may get interested in seeing what you have on the sale will click on the link.

Check the Available Categories to Know Which Is Best for Your Products

Groups are organized, so that related items end up together. Things like tables, beds, cupboards, and shoe racks end up in one category as furniture, and hence, one looking for a bed will go straight to that category. Each item on sale should fall in the group it fits best depending on what or where it is used. Some things can fall in more than one category and still meet buyers. If yours is like this, it's good to post them in all the categories they fit in so that more searches can direct clients to them. For example, sunglasses can be used for medical purposes as well as for beauty. Someone in need of sunglasses for beauty might search in the 'beauty' category. Another who may have been advised by a doctor might most probably search in the 'health' category. If as a seller you have yours posted in both categories, you will most likely have the two people view your Ad. However, be careful that your products don't fall in the wrong category. If this happens, no search will direct potential buyers to your product, and you don't want that. It can also risk your account of being blacklisted or even blocked.

Offer Free Gifts

It's in the nature of people to like free things. Depending on your product, get something you can give for free. Something related to the product will attract more buyers to view your advert, and it becomes easier to sell to them if they reach out to you. For example;

- Someone who sells ladies' clothes can consider giving free branded beauty accessories;
- A hairdresser can consider free hair clips as an after service;
- A shoe seller might consider a free pair of slippers or socks;
- Someone who sells machines can offer free assembling of the same.

It's wise to ensure that the word 'FREE' comes out legibly in the advert. If possible, the font should be more significant and color different to catch more attention. For example,

*Buy a pair of shoes and get a pair of socks for **free***

You can also have a message like;

*'hey there. Thank you for contacting us, visit our shop to get your **free** pair of socks'*,

for clients who contact you.

This is necessary because, after the attractive pictures/ videos, it will be the next thing that attracts more people to click on the Ad. The cost of the item you set up for free should be covered in the profit margin gained by selling the product. Nobody wants to run their business at a loss; otherwise, the efforts won't be worth a thing. When the gift is branded with your brand name, it's a way of making your advertisement go beyond Facebook. It causes awareness to people who might not have heard of your brand or product before. It's also a way of attracting the customer to return and send more interested friends and family your way.

Use as Many Keywords in Your Advert as Possible

When looking for a particular item to buy online, different people usually search in various engines using different words. It's good to know the keywords generally used by people searching for the product you want to sell. Make maximum use of them in your title and description. This will ensure that many relevant searches will land potential clients on your product. For instance, people who want to buy tables may use words like;

- Wooden table;
- Office table;
- Rectangle table;
- Second-hand table.

A seller with a description that captures, *'a second-hand rectangle table suitable for office use'* is most likely to be reached by all the above searches.

When more people see the Ad, one objective will have been met. It will cause traffic to your product, which is good enough. Since most people are searching the item with intentions of buying, the chances that you will make sales once they get in touch with you are high.

Offer Shipping Services Where Possible

Before a client concludes on the purchase, he /she will most probably consider how the product will reach them. Many online shoppers either don't have the time or don't want the struggle of having to transport things after buying. Most of them will buy from a seller who has delivery services, either free or at a fee. It is, therefore, a good idea to indicate availability or possibility of delivery services to maintain more clients on your wall. For clients who are from different cities, it's good that you know the courier companies available for their locations. Make sure you understand their charges so that you give instant delivery details when they ask. It is also good to be flexible to accommodate the customer's preference if they have a courier company in mind. Once the sale has been confirmed, it is again necessary to ensure you deliver in good time to avoid disappointments. Timely delivery will give you more return customers as well as referrals since it helps build confidence.

Get Ways to Make People Refer Customers to You

As a seller, you alone cannot send enough awareness to everybody. You need your Facebook friends and previous buyers to link you to their friends. You can make people refer others to you by using the following tactics;

1. Copy your link and send to your friends requesting them to share with their friends;
2. Appreciate those who refer people to you by giving them small gifts;
3. Ask people who have already bought from you to like your page and share with their friends;
4. Give a considerable discount to return customers and to those that prefer their loved ones to you. This way, you will create chains of different customers;
5. Give exceptionally good services to all your customers to keep them coming back. Happy customers will also preach it to their friends.

People who have been referred to you have more confidence in your product. For this reason, the more referrals you get, the better for your business.

Give Promo Codes to Be Redeemed at Your Shop

A promo code is given randomly with attractive discounts to lure customers. People who have a promo code will most probably show up at the shop to redeem it, and that's a sale. You can give codes redeemable within specified periods to keep clients coming. The codes also make more people visit your wall regularly to see when you have new promos. Some will refer their friends to your wall any time they see the promo running. We already know most of the referred customers will end up buying. When there are more views on your products, it's likely to translate to more sales, which is our primary objective.

Most people go through their Facebook wall for fun or looking to pass time. This is what causes traffic on Facebook throughout day and night. You can take advantage of this fact as a seller and make them notice your product. Using the above tips, any business advertising on Facebook will get easily noticed. When Ads attract clients to your wall, it's your duty as the seller to make sales. Convince most of the people that contact you to either buy instantly or come back later. Ensure that most of them also refer others to you by giving excellent customer service. This will keep your chain growing and ensure an increase in the number of sales as time goes by.

CHAPTER 2: PROVEN CASE STUDIES ON THE EFFECTIVENESS OF FACEBOOK ADS

Before you start implementing anything in your business, it is always important to validate the quality of the tool that you wish to implement. This way, you can feel confident that you are going to gain the value that you desire out of the tool that you plan on implementing.

To help you feel more confident in the power of Facebook advertising, as well as to show you just how valuable this tool can really be, let's take a look at four different case studies that prove the effectiveness of Facebook ads. This way, you can see exactly what Facebook ads can do for you and how you can use them to improve your online revenue.

Case Study #1: Facebook Ad Retargeting Creates $5,800 Monthly Recurring Revenue

This particular case study was incredible as it offered the company a whopping $5,800 per month in recurring revenue from their Facebook advertisements. Design Pickle is a company that designs unlimited graphics for companies using a monthly retainer fee. This particular company found it to be somewhat challenging to promote their business using standard practices, so they decided to try Facebook advertisements.

Through Facebook advertisements the company offered the equivalent of a free trial, with no credit card required in order for customers to get started. The free product that customers could get was a single graphic designed for their business. They began to use leads to retarget advertisements, which enables them to market specifically to people who had already landed on their page. Through this, more than 50% of their new customers signed on from Facebook advertisements alone. This lead to $5,800 recurring monthly revenue from their advertisements.

Case Study #2: $14,114 Revenue From Facebook Advertisements

In this case, a company was able to generate massive amounts of leads which lead to $14,114 in revenue from their advertisements. The company SamCart used Facebook ads to sell their courses. In these Facebook advertisements the company spent $8240 on advertisements and made $14,114 in revenue.

That's a whopping $5,874 in revenue from courses through Facebook advertisements alone.

Case Study #3: 122 Subscriptions Sold with $2.5k Ad Budget in 2 Weeks

Veeroll is a B2B company that was using Facebook advertisements to share video advertisements with their target audience. Veeroll launched a webinar and enrolled people from Facebook into the webinar through a landing page which was used to convert followers. The company ended up spending $2,500 in 2 weeks and sold 122 subscriptions out of the webinar conversion model. This resulted in $11,000 of monthly revenue, or $8,500 in profit after just two weeks.

Case Study #4: $163,969 Revenue in Just 34 Days

This particular case study was a remarkable one that lead to the company earning a massive $163,969 in revenue in just 34 days with a mere $5,989 investment. That's a $157,980 profit after just 34 days, and using a tiny fraction of the overall cost to get there.

This case was run by an advertising tech, Paul Romando, who acted on behalf of an unnamed company which was kept private for confidentiality reasons. With that being said, he returned more than 1,150 checkouts for his customer which lead to the massive income from the investment. This experience lad to a 2737.80% return on the investment in just over a month.

To create this particular ad format, Paul used a Facebook funnel which first lead customers to a lead magnet, or an opt in project that customers could check out. After that, there would be a different ad set shown to those who signed up for the opt in that was designed to take the individuals directly to a sales page. From there, they would advance through even higher ranks of products until they reached the "top tier" of products available through that company. This particular funnel is what helped Paul create such a massive return for the company he was working with.

CHAPTER 3: HOW BRANDS CAN USE CUSTOMER TESTIMONIALS TO CREATE EFFICIENT FACEBOOK AD FUNNEL

Over time, there has been a rapid increase in the cost and demand for Facebook advertising. This increase is after the realization that Facebook is the best platform to meet all types of potential buyers since most people use the app. However, Facebook Ads have increasingly lost their initial influence on buyers. This loss is due to an increased number of marketers leading to high competition. Among the audience on Facebook are some that are cold, some warm, and others hot. A sales-based Ad may not lure the cold audience into buying. A cold audience needs to be natured through awareness from being a stranger to becoming a buyer. An already warm audience that is familiar with your products requires a different approach altogether. To balance the audience, any marketer will need to build an Ad funnel.

An ad funnel is a series of campaigns that allow the marketer to deliver results from across all types of audience. A proper funnel has the following stages;

- Awareness stage;

- Consideration stage where the audience begins to build interest;

- Decision-making stage where they decide they want to buy;

- Buying stage.

At the awareness stage, the main aim is to catch the attention of the audience and earn your brand recognition. The audience at this stage can most probably be lured by the use of a video that is interesting and educative. The main aim is to catch the attention of more viewers who do not know about the product. Once the audience gets the awareness, a cold audience warms up and somehow appreciates the need for your product. At this point, some will research more about the product and even contact you for details. Some will want to buy it immediately while others will take time to think about it and may need further convincing. When building an Ad funnel, testimonials from previous customers are an essential ingredient. Here are some of the benefits of customer testimonials:

Testimonials Help in Building Trust in Potential Buyers

If a company employee tells a client how good their product is, the client will most likely not consider it seriously. This attitude is because they assume, he/she is just doing his/her job. However, if another buyer tells the same customer of how good the same product is, he/she will most likely consider purchasing it. This change of attitude is because customer testimonials are considered neutral and unbiased, in that a customer and not a business owner talks about the product. When the audience have already known about the existence of your product, some might be reluctant to buy. The reasons for being reluctant may vary. Some won't buy the product immediately because they don't know you, or they don't understand the product. Even so, some won't buy it because they don't trust you. Most people are not so fast in trusting strangers or products sold by strangers. In this case, a testimonial from someone who has interacted with you and used your product may work well in making viewers trust you. Even though the two are strangers, a person looking forward to buying your products is easily convinced by other customers. They tend to believe other customers will be honest and therefore trust what they say. With a good number of people having trust in your products, you are sure you will make a considerable number of sales.

They Work Well as A Selling Technique

Since they are not written in the seller's opinion, anyone who sees the testimonials will get interested in knowing more about you and your product. By using testimonials in the form of text, audios, and video forms on your website, people who might have never known about your product may learn about it then. The good thing is that they will hear about it from someone who has used the merchandise and not the seller. They will, therefore, get the idea of how useful the product is and might consider trying it out. Other buyers have heard about the product before but are reluctant to get it. They also get the feeling that the product is meant to help them in certain areas of their life. By this, you will save on advertisement cost. The testimonial will do enough advertisement. Needless to say, a testimonial is likely to be more convincing for decision making compared to an ordinary ad. This is because of the confidence built through the fact that the product has been helpful to other people.

They Help Viewers with A Better Understanding of The Product

Some people will see a product tagged for sale but not understand what it is or how helpful it can be. The reason behind this is most people going through Facebook will not take time to read long posts about a product. For such a client, a brief testimonial highlighting how helpful the product was gives them an idea of what it is. For example, if an image shows two photos of the same person, it will get her interested. At a closer look, she will realize the person has pimples in one image and has smooth skin on the other. She will at that point most probably conclude that the product helped clear the pimples. Having done that, they have viewed and started building interest in the product. In the instance that they have the same problems or know someone who has the same problem, they will start weighing on whether to buy or not. [Decision-making stage].

In the instance that your product had more than one benefits, different testimonials will highlight various benefits. By that, people that view them might gain interest in respect to either of the benefits. People who would have otherwise feared to try the product will get more reason to want to try it and refer friends who might benefit from the product too. Potential buyers get most of the product details and familiarize themselves with the product through the testimonials, making it easy for them to make a decision. When such customers get in touch with the seller, they usually come to buy rather than to enquire.

They Work Well in Maintaining Previous Buyers

Buyers feel more confident when they see other people recommend products they are already using. It makes them feel they made the right choice by purchasing it and will most likely become routine customers. When customers see their testimonials feature in the business ads, they feel appreciated and get the feeling of brand ownership. These people become your brand ambassadors, even beyond Facebook. The clients become loyal to your business and increase their emotional bond with it. Loyal clients also refer to other potential buyers by word of mouth.

On the other hand, some buyers who probably had tried the product but did not see results can feel very disappointed. If they don't get reasons convincing enough, they may not want to come back to your shop. However, such customers can be maintained through testimonials. For instance, some products, such as beauty products do not show results instantly and might require constant use to show tangible results. In such a case, already disappointed customers might be hard to convince that the product is good. They can only understand how it works when they see testimonials of people who had used the same and gotten results. These testimonials give them the confidence to want to try the same again, this time with a more positive attitude.

Testimonials Can Overcome Negative Incites

When it comes to social media, sellers cannot control the views of different buyers. Some people will write nasty comments on particular ads, probably because the product did not meet their expectations. Some will comment badly out of malice, while some competitors will want to paint a bad picture of you. When it comes to the audience, most people will scroll to see what other people think about the product. Several good testimonials can help repair damages caused by the negative comments on the post. In this case, it is wise to select an outstanding testimonial that refers to the product in question. In this case, a good testimonial must;

- Highlight the product's benefits;

- Tally with what you have indicated in your advert;

- Come from someone who can be identified;

- Prove that your product is the best.

They Play A Big Role in The Conversion Rate

Through the ads funnel, the audience is converted from a total stranger to a buyer. Most Facebook users who come across the ads are not on Facebook to search for products on sale. They will most probably not buy immediately they see an advertisement. Catchy videos that display testimonials are a good way of making them notice your Ads and click on them. Once they click on the video and watch to the end, they are able to get some crucial information about the product. The presence of good testimonials is what will lead them to consider visiting your website. At the site, their main agenda will be to see the product being referred to in the testimonials. This category of clients goes through the funnel stages and get convinced faster through the testimonials than through what they would have seen in an ordinary advert. Credit goes to the testimonies, first for introducing the product with confidence that it surely is good, and for proving that it has been tested. Studies have shown that most online buyers decided to buy after going through several customer testimonials.

It Creates A Positive Reputation for Your Product and Business

Keenly selected testimonials from your customers create a good image of your product, more strongly than what you state in your ads. Consequently, this gives more customers a vivid good picture of your product and business. As an end product, they erase any doubt about the product being of good help to them.

Testimonials also help in giving a clear difference between your product and your business from that of your competitors. Besides, once a good reputation is created to the society about your product, the chances of attracting new customers and maintaining the current ones rise. When many customers like your products and give testimonials, chances of the product brand going viral increase. When a product goes viral for a good reason, positive returns are recorded, which is the main aim at the end of the day. The beauty of a good reputation is that it gets more people to want the association with the product. It also makes it easy to post your Ad on different sites and increase the product's awareness.

When your product has a good reputation, fans share about it on their social media platforms. Their friends, family, and colleagues will learn about you through them and most likely want to know more about the product. They will be marketing your product as they take pride in it.

They Help to Increase the Credibility of Your Brand

While big brands are already known to clients in the whole region, sellers with unknown brands have the task of making them known for them to be competitive. Most buyers are skeptical about the credibility of a product when they first see it in an advert. Testimonials from customers help with this by creating social proof. When people see testimonials of your customers on your website, they relax at the fact that other people know about you. Many people feel that since someone else has used a particular brand and says it is good, then it must be good. Most customers rate the credibility of a product or business, depending on the number of people who talk about it. They use this measure of credibility to determine whether they buy from marketer A or B. A company that has products of lesser quality but has many people talking about it will seem more credible. This is in comparison to one with excellent quality but few people talking about it. It's therefore evident that people trust what other people think about a brand than what they know about it. With this fact in mind, well-selected testimonials should feature on your website, citing beautiful photos of happy customers and good reviews. The more the testimonials featuring a brand or item, the better for the business. By doing this, you increase the credibility of your product, build a chain of customers, and make your brand competitive in the market.

Testimonials, When Used Properly, Are Very Persuasive

Most of the testimonials have stories in them which capture the attention of the audience. Because the stories are personified, they tend to create intense emotions, therefore, connecting the reader to the advert. When you connect emotionally with the audience, you can easily convince them to buy your product. Mostly they don't buy because of how they see the product but because of how they feel about the same. The language used is also persuasive because it is universal and in the voice of another buyer and not the seller. Visual aspects in the testimonials bring out more emotions, and they come out in a way more convincing than any other part of an advert. All a business person needs to know is how best they can use testimonials given by their satisfied customers to persuade possible buyers to become real buyers.

The above-mentioned points prove that business people should use customer testimonials to create efficient Facebook Ads. This is based on the fact that testimonials have proven to be a very strong convincing factor. They have also proven to help businesses increase traffic on their sites. With the need for every business to stand out, sellers cannot afford to ignore an essential detail as such. It is, therefore, advisable for every business person who has exceeded the expectations of his clients to request them to write testimonials. From the various testimonials, you are able to get, you incorporate specific ones for particular adverts. When choosing testimonials for a Facebook ad, it's recommended that you use an affirmative testimony that is likely to catch the attention of any random Facebook user. Many people get attracted more to videos and images as compared to texts. Testimonials in terms of videos and pictures will, therefore, be a better option for use in any Facebook ad. The reason they are mostly preferred is because they can show real emotions, body language, and audios at the same time. This tactic works well in making the emotional connection possible. Video Testimonials also help brands reach through masses of people who are of different language groups. Even though some cannot understand the language used in the advert, they can view images and watch videos to get the context. With the clients' testimonials acting as advertisement Medias, they help in cutting costs on commercial adverts. This use of testimonials reduces the expenditure of the business but rises the income through sales.

CHAPTER 4: OPTIMIZING FACEBOOK ADS

Facebook is an online social media networking platform that allows people all over the world to communicate and interact with one another. It is one of the leading platforms in the world that has enabled people around the world to feel closer to different parts of the globe.

With this in mind, Facebook, the social media giant has optimized its operations by creating promotion options such as Facebook ads. These options allow business owners to sponsor their preferred posts and cover a broad market. The ads can either feature Business posts, motivational posts, religious posts, and sports. With an efficient ad, there is no doubt that any company can reach the target market with little resources.

Nowadays, business firms can use different categories or types of ads given to promote their products on Facebook. These can be categorized into four groups, namely:

1. Traffic Improvement Ads;
2. Consumers Appreciation Ads;
3. New products ads;
4. Lead ads.

a. Traffic improvements ads

Aim at improving the number of customers that can see a product that has been advertised. Every business must strive always to acquire more customers.

b. Consumer Appreciation Ads

Most firms and organizations, in general, always focus only on getting a customer and stopping on that once they have convinced the customer to buy their products. However, any firm should strive to make a onetime customer a regular customer. That's why Facebook offers this ad to enable a company to appreciate their customers.

c. New Product Ads

This category of ads allows a firm to sponsor and advertise a new product to its targeted audience or consumers.

d. Leads Ad

This type of ads enables a customer to optimize his or her contacts with the company to receive ads at any time. It allows business owners to reach out to the right market without having to dig deep into their pockets.

Optimizing Facebook ads means that a sponsored post on Facebook gives the most successful output from the targeted audience. This book looks at some of the techniques an organization can use to get the most successful result from a Facebook sponsored post.

Here's how business owners can Optimize Facebook ads;

1. **Being Distinct**

   A firm targeting to run an ad should always focus on being specific on what they are about to advertise. First, they should be specific on a product they are about to advertise, be distinct on the consumers they are targeting and also specify the target age bracket of the consumer they are focusing on. For instance, when it comes to a product to do with small babies, the company's focus should be on females aged between 16-35 since, at this age bracket, many ladies have babies. When a product is mostly targeting the youths, then it would be advisable for a firm to select a certain age group so as to reach the optimum target market. This is even easy because Facebook gives you all the options that you need.

2. **Investing in Video Ads**

   Video ads and animations also play a big role in attracting more customers and keeping those that already exist. Just like cartoons, video ads are attractive and will always make your target consumers more likely to follow the ads. These videos should not be necessarily expensive but should be of high quality and well-produced to avoid embarrassments that may create loopholes in the overall marketing campaign. With video ads on Facebook, one is assured of good and optimum results that will be of big benefit to the business.

3. Maximizing on Potential Customers Who Visit Your Website

Most competitive firms are always able to know those who visit their sites either by following their IP addresses or by even offering pop up for the visitors to subscribe. A firm may use this advantage by making these people their target market when doing an ad on Facebook. These people are normally the first people to see the sponsored post when it is posted on Facebook. This might help in convincing a customer who had visited the site and not made his or her mind on purchasing a particular product or service. This tactic is always useful as a back up to convince a customer and finalize a deal.

4. Understanding the Target Group

This means that a marketer should be able to understand those who'll access the advertisement. For instance, a marketer should know the target group that is already aware of the product so that he/she should not waste resources in re-advertising to them. More energy should be focused on new potential customers.

5. Getting Detailed Information About Your Target Group

A good Facebook ad marketer should know the age and gender of the target audience. Not all audience performs the same, and hence, an ad should not ignore the important fact that even their financial power is not the same. Thanks to Facebook, business owners can easily get more information about their audience from a simple button click. Knowing the age and gender of your audience is essential, as it gives you the knowledge of what needs to be done to meet the requirements of such an audience. For instance, it would be of no use to advertise ladies' clothing to all the audiences without categorically focusing on the ladies. By taking specific audiences, this can allow one to get the optimum result that he or she requires.

6. Pick Out an Audience Depending on Their Level of Income

Facebook ads platform offers business persons a chance to pick their audience or target market in accordance with their levels of income. Given that the audiences might have different levels of income, some people prefer to buy things that are highly priced while others would prefer to buy cheaper stuff. With this in mind, a marketer can maximize on by picking a specific audience in regards to their financial income. Getting the audience that prefers goods that are highly-priced would be a gold mine to the marketer or a firm because they will end up making a good profit.

7. Demographic and Climatic Conditions

Facebook ads allow business owners to choose an audience from specific demographic areas. Climatic conditions would also be considered by a marketer when advertising his or her products. For instance, it will be poor for a marketer who sells jackets and sweaters to target an audience that is in arid and dry areas. But it will be of great profitability for a marketer to target audiences in cold areas with the same products they will highly sell. Given that Facebook is almost all over the world, the marketer can easily divide his/her audiences in accordance with their demographic surroundings.

8. Scheduling Your Ads

Facebook allows a person to schedule his or her advertisements to a time of his or her convenience. With this, a firm will be able to schedule their product advertisement to a specific time that is profitable. Most businesses target to advertise when they are on their peak so that they can sell well.

9. Having a Clear Objective of The Ad

All successful businesses must always have an objective for them to thrive through the daily growing competition. Just like in a football game, every team must have an objective in every season that they play. Therefore, for one to have the best results, a marketer must always have specific or several objectives before running an advertisement on Facebook. A person must well know what he or she would love to achieve after running an advertisement. With that in mind, one is sure of getting the best result he or she expected.

10. Designing Your Facebook Ads

Given that audiences will tend to use different gadgets when accessing their Facebook account, it is prudent for a marketer to design his or her ad for both the phone layout and personal computer layout. This will help in maintaining the attractiveness of the advertisement in both gadgets. One should also make sure that the advertisement is in the right place where it can easily be seen by the target audience. Also, consider the Facebook marketers budget that he or she is willing to use for the advertisement process. One should not choose a budget that he or she is cannot manage. With the practice of the above-mentioned points, businesses can use the ideas to have optimum final results after running an ads Facebook ad. Facebook is a great platform, and every marketer should utilize it to reach the target audience with much ease. It saves on the amount of money that would be spent if the marketing is done physically.

Facebook Ads Techniques

1. Objectives

This is the most important aspect before even running an ad on your Facebook. One must at least have clear objectives or goals that he or she is considering to achieve after running the advertisement. In normal life, for one to succeed in doing anything he/she must first what he/she wants to gain from it. Objectives basically are the basis of every successful task that one might have. Having these objectives helps one understand what action the audience will take once they see the advertisement at first glance.

The first objective that a successful advertisement should have is creating awareness. Your audience must at least familiarize yourself with the products or services that you offer.

Another important objective is having conversions. For instance, most marketers would wish to make their audience to go to their website. To do this, your ad would probably have an incentive such as a discount to your customers. To make them go to your website, you should not give out a discount code to your customers before they go to your website. You should put a structure that takes them to step by step to your website where they, for instance, insert their emails before getting the discount code. With this, you will have the upper hand in that at least you will have the customer's contacts, and you can communicate with them from time to time.

2. Setting Up Your Audience

The second step of having a successful Facebook ad campaign is by setting up the ideal customized audience that you prefer.

Focusing is essential in your campaign and how you focus can either make your ad perform perfectly or fail terribly.

Some of the things to look at when choosing your audience will include;

a. Location

First, you must have a location where your audience to be that is in accordance with what your product line is. For instance, if you are from Africa and your products are arts and crafts and African indigenous crafts that attracts tourists it would be prudent for you to set a location where most tourists come from, and that is basically the west of Europe. With that, you are more likely to get more audience in Europe compared to Africa where the audience will not be so much. Basically, setting up the most suitable audience would be a great step in making the advertisement very successful.

b. Age

This is another essential step in getting the right audience with Facebook ads; one is able to choose his most appropriate audience age in line with the product that he deals in. For instance, if the product you are dealing with is mostly fashion, it will be prudent for one to focus on the young generation that is the youths between let's say 15-35. It will be of no use to focus your advertisement of the latest clothing fashion and swag to the older age for they are prone to ignore the advertisement.

c. Gender

Gender should also be considered when running advertisements on Facebook. Different genders prefer different products hence the gender that you target should go in line with the product that you sell. Facebook ads offer a marketer the choice to choose the gender that they would prefer to reach. For example, it will be of importance to choose the female gender when dealing with ladies such as earrings, lipsticks, etc.

d. Language

This is another important perspective to consider. The language that you use during advertisements should go well with the target audience that you will pick. Given that we have different languages in the world, a good marketer should choose a language that is well understood by his/her target audience with ease.

Other factors to consider would be; interest, the behavior of your audience. For instance, if your business deals with events organizing such as weddings, you should as well choose the audience who have an interest in weddings or birthday parties.

Finance is another factor that should be factored a good market must choose the budget that he or she is well convenient with.

Testing Your Ad

This is the final step for one to have a very successful Facebook ad campaign. One should at least first test his or her ad before it goes live on air. Thanks to Facebook, one has an opportunity to test his ad before it starts showing live. This helps a promoter or marketer to see how the ad will appear in phones, personal computers, and other gadgets that the audience might use.

This is where the marketer customizes his or her ad by choosing the themes, pictures, videos, or music that he or she would prefer to use to run the advert. Most importantly, the success of a Facebook advertisement will depend on marketer's strategy and the most important objectives. The most effective strategy that is always preferred is by creating multiple ads that categorically explain your products and services. For instance, you can create an ad that contains multiple images, videos, and a fine-tune audio sound.

The success of your advertisement will depend deeply on the strategies that a firm or individual use to advertise their products, choosing the right audience, gender, location and interest of your target market can be of great help and can easily make a Facebook ad campaign successful and productive and achieve optimum results.

In general, Facebook has proven to be a great platform where businesses can be promoted and even sales made. Most firms have used it, and the platform is growing day by day as a profitable platform to do business. It is a platform that if well utilized, it can lead to successful business growth and an increase in sales.

Apart from influential business people, celebrities, celebrated artists use it to promote their ideas, songs, and concept. From this, it's clearly evident that Facebook ads have the main objective of promoting market areas and audiences around the globe as a whole.

CHAPTER 5: A STEP BY STEP GUIDE ON CREATING FACEBOOK ADS THAT ARE EFFICIENT AND REVENUE SAVING

With the emergence of several marketing strategies today, Facebook is one of the platforms used in creating enticing advertisements. The chapter highlights a step by step guide on building productive and efficient Facebook Ads essential for your business management plans.

Subsequently, there are different methods used to create Facebook Ads in plenty of books, but this one encompasses the most efficient and revenue saving. Facebook Ads may take various forms depending on the type of advertisement displayed. Each step discussed in the book entails descriptive details of the necessities to ensure the creation of Ads suitable for the vast market. More so, the book provides additional information for the benefit of creating productive outcomes.

The first step is always crucial as such; the chapter introduces the most critical information to ensure the following steps become successful. The concept adopted to generate the guide on creating Facebook Ads that are efficient and revenue saving is dependable and can be put into action immediately. The following steps primarily follow the previous ones precisely to avoid confusion. The last step, therefore, gives you the go-ahead to implement the best Facebook Ads for your audience.

Step 1: Creating Your Facebook Business Manager Account

Facebook account is another thing, and Facebook business manager account is another one is used for your business while another is just for socializing. Setting up a Facebook business manager account is the initial step to ensure the creation of a more sophisticated campaign. Unlike many e-commerce platforms, Facebook business manager houses all your details, including ads, customizing tools, and business pages for ease maneuver within your Facebook Ads strategy. You may also download Facebook pixels to manage your ads, which some users find it very essential to monitor ads' progress.

Creation of a Facebook business manager account provides the first step to the nature of Facebook Ads that are efficient and revenue saving. Visit business.facebook.com and click on Create Account. You will then submit your business name, Facebook business page, title, and email address. Fill then spaces and add advertising account through clicking Business Manager Menu and selecting Business Settings. Click Account and Ad Account and create or add an advertising account.

Step 2: Select the Right Objective

Facebook comprises of more than two billion monthly users henceforth attracting several brands to Facebook Ads as a means of marketing their products and services. The first thing to conduct before engaging in creating Facebook Ads is to choose a specific objective to fit into a given category of your campaign. Facebook initially asks you to select your purpose during the first step of developing your Facebook Ads manager. Choosing the right objective also enables you to focus on Facebook marketing techniques while yielding well-tailored results.

There are three types of objectives which include awareness, consideration, and conversion, guiding you correctly to your needs. Awareness focuses solely on brand recognition and reaches your audiences both on products and content. Objectives under considerations create traffic, product engagement, and provision of messages, therefore, generating interest for your audience to search for your brand. Conversions are objectives that enable your audience to get an urge to purchase your products through catalog sales, store sales, and conversions.

As such, awareness objectives are essential for campaigns and promotion of new businesses and you readily reach new potential customers. Conversion and store visits are crucial for increasing physical sales while narrowing down to more specific objectives, for instance, video views and mobile app installs. After selecting your preferred target and understand your goals, you are now aware of what you want to achieve in your Facebook advertisement.

Step 3: Select the Right Audience

Facebook has more than two billion active users of different ages, demography, varying interests, and distributed globally. It is therefore essential to narrow down to those relevant to the content displayed from the daily active users. Facebook offers three crucial sources of generating audiences; core, custom, and lookalike, which enable you to focus and determine your desired target audience. Most e-commerce brands utilize these three sources to create a successful marketing strategy across significant advertising platforms, including Facebook.

Core Audiences

The format of selecting your core audiences include a manual selection of groups according to your criterion, for instance, behavioral, likes, interests, and location characteristic. Interests and equivalents such as exercises relate to contents already existing on active user Facebook accounts and what they have interacted together. Behaviors comprise of certain activities or actions undertaken by users and stored by Facebook. Location includes specific user immediate environments while demographics entail profile information such as engineers.

Custom Audiences

Custom audiences include uploading contact lists of your current or former customers to engage with your target audience.

Audience customization is one of the easiest, and your customers may provide testimonies about the physical activities of your brand. The details are then matched with users, and the ads remain delivered to target audiences directly. It, therefore, provides information about new products or product changes as well as reaching them through email addresses.

Lookalike Audiences

Lookalike audiences are ideal users you never engaged but generated from finding people similar to your existing audience. They can also be created from custom audiences selected from the specific population and may depend on location or specified criteria. Lookalike audiences increase over time from small percentages and may include new users who get into contact with your brand and access your goods and services physically.

Selecting a specific audience for your Facebook Ads ensures that your marketing strategy has a better chance of growing. More so, you can easily engage with past, existing, and targeted audiences, therefore, creating more room for converting your ads. Other categories of determining your audience include location-based, connection targeting, and demographics. The technique enables the ads to show to users both connected to your brand or not. Lookalike audiences remain the most reliable source used to attract your audience to your business website. It uses existing information to create new prospective clients.

Step 4: Choose Where to Display Your Ads

Facebook offers a wide range of platforms to display your ads for the benefit of reaching your specified audience. At the ad set level, you are free to choose where to you want your ads to show, including placements, devices, and other Facebook-owned platforms. Devices may include the ad to display on mobile only, desktop-only or both while also displaying on Instagram or messenger or both. Facebook also owns multiple apps where you can select where you want to show your ads.

However, Facebook recommends advertisers to choose an automated placement method to customize and optimize ads to produce the best outcome. You can also decide to whom you want the information to reach and select your desired audience. For example, if your target audiences are frequent mobile users, then choosing Instagram and Facebook messenger are the most reliable choices for your Facebook Ads display platforms. You may also select different groups depending on your product services while hindering your brand from showing to irrelevant groups.

Step 5: Set Your Budget Limit

Facebook provides different options for optimizing the cost of an advertising campaign. Choosing your budget includes selecting how frequent you wish your ads to display in chosen platforms. Facebook Ads may show daily, occasionally or lifetime running either indefinitely or as scheduled. Your optimization of how the ads will run will, therefore, determine the cost you are to incur during the advertising period.

Facebook Ads performance and auctions are also other indicators of how the success and the cost may vary, especially when your audience view your adverts. However, it is crucial to set your auction into automated for those not aware of how such bids work. Similarly, you may set specific parameters in the previous steps which may exceed or overweigh what you expected. Setting some limitations during deciding your budget is essential in providing solutions to high costs during your campaign.

Besides, you can easily optimize your Ads manually as Facebook offers automated parameters which you may need to update. Thus, you can easily add, eliminate, or change some features which may alter your budget either becoming higher or lower than expected. For a successful Facebook Ads campaign, it is essential to set a favorable budget while maximizing on attracting new audiences in your brand.

Sometimes budgeting for your ads may accompany multiple challenges, but privacy and confidentiality of your information remain guaranteed of safety by Facebook. Set your budgets well to avoid additional charges as indicated in the creative dialogue. Budgeting for displaying Facebook ads is not only determined by the audience of whom your products are intended, but also depend on the following factors;

- Length of display of advertisements in the system;

- Extend of ads to related platforms;

- Cost of your products;

- Customer acquisition costs.

Step 6: Select Your Format

Displaying ads on Facebook offers a range of formats suitable for your advertisements and more so allowing you to select the right format. The forms provide Facebook among the most effective and reliable for any campaign. You can quickly choose the format fitting your objective and the targeted audience while within your budget. Some of the ad's formats provided include;

- Single image;

- Video format;

- Canvas;

- Slideshows;

- Collection;

- Carousel.

Each format comes with its benefits; for instance, photos provide a unique story for your audience compared to videos which provide a deeper engagement with sounds, images, and motions. Carousel is similar to videos but may lack sound and display in an image manner while collections display your products and the story behind it. Links ads direct your audience to your websites. Dynamics showcase your product in a more sophisticated way, and canvas ads are essential for providing full-screen displays primarily for mobile devices. Slideshows are the most affordable and offer a lightweight motion.

Slideshows, video, and carousel ads are among the best formats to market your brand and products as they have the maximum engagement and CTR rates compared to other forms. However, it is vital to select the best format for your ad to avoid increased costs of advertising while creating a broader audience. Facebook usually offer the best options of sizes while the company may guide you on some of the formats to rely on during your format selection.

Step 7: Adding Crucial Data and Placing Your Ad

Facebook ads are quite different compared to previous advertising techniques used in e-commerce marketing strategies. When using the Facebook business manager, you will need to select a business page or an Instagram account which you wish to use to present your campaign. Dynamic of products is one of the critical elements which connects your Facebook pixel and Facebook product catalog. Therefore, users or followers can view similar products you have added in your ads account. The technique enables you to retarget your advertisements through Facebook's dynamic products.

The creation of connections between your business website, ad account, Facebook pixel, and Facebook business manager enables the development of a more dynamic campaign, in achieving your objective quickly. Dynamics product ads are also essential for prospecting, enabling Facebook to display other products relevant to your brand even when not in the ad. Dynamic products campaign, therefore, increased your advertising plans while primarily connecting all your marketing platforms.

During filling of the dialogue, there may exist small details with crucial information that you miss while filling in different areas. Some include URL description and other selections at the creative collection. As such, take advantage and fill them with the CTA option and true copy playing a significant role in your advertising campaign through Facebook Ads. Then confirm all the information provided, including payments, targeted audience, and format before submitting and placing your order.

Step 8: Optimization of Your Ad Performance

Facebook Ad monitoring and measurement of its performance is an essential aspect as it enables you to analyze if it meets your objectives. Some campaigns may witness immediate CPC while others may begin to grow after the increase in the frequency of visits. Similarly, others may fail to perform as expected henceforth may demand effort. However, Facebook's ads manager will display all active campaigns within your profile.

Henceforth enabling you to click and monitor any campaign you wish to analyze its progress or make changes.

Some of the activities to check to include relevant scores, actions taken by your audience after viewing the ad, frequency, and CPC value. It is also recommended that you check on your Facebook Ads daily for the benefit of analyzing your daily logs. There are situations where you may fail to experience any sale within a day or two. Hence, it is essential to be patient instead of turning off your ads or make changes. The algorithms may show a different outcome, but people may get attracted to your products over time.

Investing in Funneling

Creation of a funnel during product marketing through Facebook Ads entail an understanding that the majority of your audience will buy your product over time rather than immediately. Funnel-based strategies enable you to tailor your ad according to the audience's interests to purchase and familiarize yourself with your brand. In Facebook ads, creating a funnel allows you to reach quiet audiences of potential clients in a given campaign as well as those visiting your website without making a purchase.

The funnel also enables you to create more content-based advertisements suiting your budget, thus being intricate while covering a more comprehensive range of campaigns. Funneling, therefore, creates more prospective room to gain more sales in your brand but remains crucial in selecting a less expensive strategy. Besides, the funnel enables Facebook ads and each audience to acquire different methods of creative designs bringing prospects essential to drive purchases on your website.

Using Facebook Ads in Ecommerce Marketing Strategies

Since the introduction of Facebook business manager, Facebook advertising has created a favorable platform for different brands to grow and reach more clients. Using the account encompasses different groups of people, including those with no experience within the digital marketing sector. Facebook ads have become more attractive as reaching more targeted has been simplified significantly.

Facebook advertising is cheaper, faster, and business owners can readily check the progress of their ads and make necessary changes where applicable. As such, learning the basics of Facebook advertisement enables you to set up your account correctly and establish a successful campaign henceforth growing your business. With different forms to choose from, Facebook ads will work in your benefit as long as you have a working plan and the development of a stronger ad.

CHAPTER 6: WHY BRANDS USE FACEBOOK ADS TO MAXIMIZE SALES

Modern-day marketing has shifted to digital as compared to traditional analog forms of marketing. Digital marketing techniques include blogging, affiliate marketing, email marketing, and SEO marketing. Social media sites such as Facebook, Instagram, Twitter, and WhatsApp form the platforms for internet marketing. Of all these sites, Facebook is the most popular one and boasts of over 2.5 billion users daily. Studies show that 60% of buyers are influenced by Facebook when making both offline and online purchases. This fact makes the leading site for digital marketing as it guarantees to reach a wider audience.

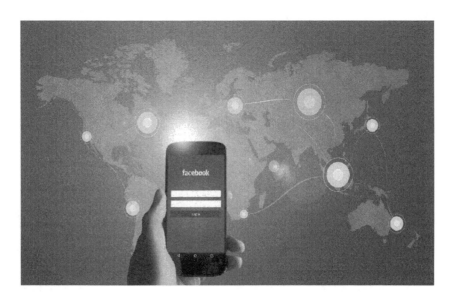

It is inevitable for brands not to use Facebook ads to survive in the modern market as a means of maximizing sales and targeting the right audience. The reasons for this are explained below.

1. **People spend a good amount of time on Facebook**

   Facebook is the king of all social media sites. The average Facebook user spends a little above 1 hour on Facebook every single day just reading content and liking posts. Most of these users use mobile devices. These are your potential clients, and the fact that they spend a considerable amount of time on Facebook is really important for you to use Facebook ads. It is during this time that they can come across your brand, and depending on what you are offering and their preferences, some might just become interested! Remember, there is strength in numbers, and Facebook provides these numbers quite easily.

2. **Affordability**

   Facebook advertising is a very affordable means of advertising. It is possible to reach a large group of people but spends very little money. It has a relatively low cost per action. For this reason, it would be wiser to utilize it as compared to placing commercials on television and radio, which could cost you an arm and a tooth. You can use as low as 50$ and reach 50000 people. You can also set a daily or lifetime budget which you can adjust at any given time.

The cost of Facebook ads is also lower than that of other digital platforms like LinkedIn and Instagram. In fact, the costs are cut down by up to 75%. This is unmatched.

3. You can gauge its results

The results of the ads will not be a mere estimation, but rather, they can be quantified. There are experts in Facebook advertising who can install conversion pixels on your site that come in handy to observe the activity. You will know how many people have visited your site, how many new followers who could be potential customers, how many clicks and conversions you have gotten. Therefore, it does not involve speculation like other traditional methods. It is also effective because you can know the reaction from your viewers since the ads provide a chance to express like, dislike or comment.

Moreover, if you do not see results, you can adjust your campaign, unlike in traditional methods where you cannot change tact immediately if you fail to see results.

4. Facebook ads can bring you to repeat clients

There are always the one-time clients and then those who come back, the repeat clients. Every business person's desire is to have their clients come back. You can use the audience features of such clients to add their emails into your Facebook advertising campaigns. This is because people who once bought from you are more likely to make a repeat purchase because they are users of your brand. One purchase should not be the end of the relationship between you and your buyer. Take advantage of the power of creating repeat customers.

5. **It can help increase referrals by word of mouth**

Tell a friend to tell a friend. This phrase is especially true when a customer is satisfied by the product or service that they got from you. A contented client will tell their friend and family in this case who might also become your clients. It may even go viral. Many fashion businesses have thrived this way. Someone orders a dress from a cloth store online and loves what is delivered. She will definitely tell her friends to check it out. The effect? A positive trajectory in the volume of your sales, which will, in turn, increase your profits.

6. **Your business rivals are also using Facebook advertising**

You definitely want to outsmart your competitors. It is business, and every entrepreneur is fighting to remain afloat. Your rivals are also using Facebook ads to maximize their sales. They are targeting the very audience that you are missing out on. To avoid being left behind, you cannot ignore the benefits that come with using Facebook advertising. Customers spend a considerable amount of time on Facebook, and that is exactly how you can get them.

Be sure to check out on the ads of your competitors. Make sure that yours are more compelling. Who knows? You might just sway away your competitor's biggest followers, and this may also result in sales conversion.

7. Facebook ads can be a good ground to compete with bigger brands

Start-ups can leverage internet marketing to be able to deal with competition from bigger and more established brands. You only have to make sure your ads are catchy, persuasive, and geared towards a certain audience to be able to thrive. Normally bigger brands have a bigger capital base and high profits and therefore engage inexpensive methods of advertising like television commercials and billboards, which may not be possible for new entrants.

8. You can also get clients out of Facebook platform

There are those clients who can know about your brand from elsewhere and then come to your Facebook. Through your ads, they may further visit your website and eventually come to your physical address if they are impressed with what you have to offer. Actually, Facebook has a tool that is able to track offline purchases that have been triggered by Facebook ads. People can be able to locate the nearest shop from the ad because this feature is able to show the estimated time of travel, address, and phone contacts.

9. Facebook advertisement can help you penetrate new markets

You can test the market at your own pace using Facebook advertisements for people who are considering introducing a new brand into the market. The platform will increase awareness about your brand, and people start getting interested in your product, translating into sales. Thus, it is very reliable for an entrepreneur in need of breaking into new markets.

10. Can be done anywhere

The mobile nature of Facebook advertising makes it very simple o reach the right target at their own convenience. Three-quarters of Facebook users log in using mobile phones. With the over 2. 5 million Facebook users, the potential audience will be reached. You cannot compare Facebook advertising with TV commercials where one has to literally schedule a time to watch TV so that they can watch your advert. It is therefore very versatile and can be used at any place, any time.

11. Time conscious

Facebook advertisement does not waste time. It does not take long to reach out to a large number of people. It is really encouraging for a business person to start receiving interested clients barely a few hours after placing an ad. It even boosts the enthusiasm of that person to continue selling their brand with more zeal.

12. Boosts brand awareness

The more people know about the existence of your brand, the more they are likely to buy from you. Facebook advertising will be a great way to inform the target audience about your brand, and they can then sample it and make a decision on whether to make a purchase or not.

You can boost brand awareness using Facebook ads by sharing superb content, using quora, and following influencers. Do not post the same tone and content across all channels. This could be absolutely boring. To make yourself stand out, use consistent branding in all parts of your website, and have a bio that is really appealing.

13. You can set up ads quite easily

Facebook ads are quite easy to set up. It is as simple as choosing the type of ad to set up, selecting your target group, choosing your budget, and the time needed to accomplish. You can opt to customize it from an array of formats and bidding techniques. You can pay per like, per impression, per click or per action.

14. You can have a specific target

Your potential customers can be gotten from filtering by connections, for example, friends of the users who follow your page or behavior and interests which entails people who have purchased a certain product recently. You can also filter according to location. This is for sellers targeting people of a specific geographical area. You can also filter based on marital status, gender, age, job description as long as it suits the service or products on offer.

A good example of filtering is in location targeting; you can target a specific country, state, or city. You can still filter for recent travelers to the location, people living in that location, or better still everyone in that location. Wow! How amazing.

15. Facebook provides video ads

Human beings are visual creatures. They would rather watch a video describing a brand than reading tons of information about the same brand. Video ads are also catchy and thus grab more attention. It is, therefore, a very useful marketing tool that is made possible by Facebook ads. In the end, Facebook ads drive more conversions. To make your video ads more result-oriented, make it short, have the right objective, and know your key performance indicators. Make sure that your call to action falls in the middle of the video ad.

16. Call buttons have taken it a notch higher

Call buttons have changed the game. Its effectiveness is much better than a click to a website. Thanks to call buttons, you see an ad, click on the call now button and guess what? The lead is captured. For someone using a mobile device, making a call is simpler than navigating through a website since it is a quicker way to get information. Call buttons have totally revolutionized Facebook advertising and can be termed as the most important feature so far. Amazing!

17. The power of remarketing

Remarketing is an advertising strategy that enables you to advertise to recent visitors to your website. This happens when you visit a website, and an add pops up a short while later. Someone can visit your website but fail to purchase or to contact you. You can leverage Facebook ads to engage and follow up on such customers, which will, in turn, lead to conversions.

18. Facebook ads can increase visits to your blog

Blogs are a great way to engage closely with your audience. Facebook can be a great tool to narrow the gap between traffic and your blog. Blogs tremendously grow with traffic hence the need for your blog to reach a wider audience. It should be as credible as possible for people to trust that the content is worth clicking on.

This means that it can also increase your social media followers on your social platforms. If you have email newsletters, your subscribers will also increase.

19. Your SEO rankings can be boosted

Social signals help to determine how to rank search engines. A higher SEO means you will get more traffic on your website than people who also similar keywords, therefore, gaining increased website referrals from search engines. The activity of social media; comments, shares, and likes on a post constitute social signals. Through Facebook, your social signals can be increased, meaning that your SEO rankings will also be improved.

SEO rankings greatly influence customer's decisions to buy since people considered brands with higher SEO rankings to be more credible and reliable. It is actually the latest PR strategy and should be invested in.

20. Effectiveness

There is evidence to show that Facebook marketing actually works. Research shows that over 90% of online marketers confirm that advertising via Facebook has been instrumental in ensuring that their business has been a success. The interesting part is that it does not discriminate but helps both startups and well-established businesses reach their audience, increase sales, and consequently increase their profits. Facebook's large global audience and the affordable costs render it the most effective and desired way of advertising.

21. Facebook users influence each other's decision to buy

Consumers get to talk about products in different groups on Facebook. Users of a product may talk about how they have found it in their Facebook pages. This will be important to you because first you can get to referrals out of this and you can also get negative feedback about your product, which will help you to improve.

For example, you are dealing with cooking oil; you might need to join cook groups where people who use cooking oils engage in following on their comments. You will also know the advantages your competitors have over you improve on the areas you need to. Another good example is a mom's group if you are dealing in diapers to where you will get to know about their various preferences.

22. Facebook organic reach is limited

Nowadays, having a Facebook page alone is not enough. Organic Facebook reach is fast declining because of the large content being created and recreated every single day. Less than 10% of your followers may actually follow up on your updates in their news feed because news feed has been designed first to show Facebook users news that is most relevant to them, for example, posts from their friends or their locality first. Facebook limits the visibility of business pages in the news feed. In paid promotion, many people will be to come across your brand because this limitation is overcome. You will have no option than to use ads to enable people to know about your brand.

23. Control burden lays on you

It is up to you to decide the content that is released in the ads and also how the budget plays out. You can also get to decide who sees your ads. This control is very dear to you because every business person's desire is to participate in decision making in their business and the type of ads to place is a very critical decision that will determine whether a business will succeed or fail.

Types of Business Models that Can Use Facebook Ads

Business Ownership Models

Before venturing into any business, you need to understand different business ownership structures. Investors usually decide on the type of business based on location, demand, and plan. While some business owners like getting attention, some prefer to go lowkey. Here are the four common types of business ownership models.

Sole Proprietorship

Most less capital-intensive businesses often start as sole proprietors. It is the simplest on the list and is owned by one person who may decide to use their name or not. All you need to have is a social security number and the necessary permits. This type of business is not subjected to many conflicts because the owner is the sole decision-maker. Besides, sole proprietors usually are taxed once and thus avoid any involving paperwork to operate. Most start-up businesses should go for this type of structure before they get more sophisticated. It gives them a chance to clearly understand the market dynamics before pumping in more capital or bringing in more investors on board.

Partnership

This usually arises when two or more people team up to form a joint business. There should be a formal written agreement that approves the union. Otherwise, it may be easy for one partner to contest for the ownership of that business. Partnerships come with advantages such as sharing the business start-up cost and losses. However, this kind of structure requires utmost professionalism because it can easily collapse when conflicts and arguments arise. All partners are 100% responsible for all the crucial decisions made. They also have unique tax requirements, and a lot of paperwork is required when filing for returns. Any tax evasions schemes are taken seriously and can lead to the closure of the business.

Corporation

For this structure, owners have limited liability and the business functions independently. This means that the owners are protected by the law from facing any personal legal action should the business be sued. Corporations have individual rights and are held responsible as a distinct entity. They have sophisticated tax requirements, and a lot of paperwork should be submitted while filing for tax returns.

Limited Liability Company (LLC)

LLCs are like corporations with the only difference being that they are owned by multiple individuals, trustees, corporations, and other LLCs. The owners have limited liability because LLCs are also treated as individual business entities. Under proper guidelines, LLCs can file taxes like partnerships only that there will be more paperwork.

Business ownership structures vary a lot, and you should do your research before investing in any business. It will give you a careful investment insight after weighing on the available exit options.

To sum it all up, it is time you accept that Facebook ads are needed to move your business to the next step. In fact, if you are not already using Facebook ads, you need to get started right away. The reason for this is because of the large number of people that use Facebook, the ability to remarket that Facebook offers, the wonder that is the call button feature and the ability to reach a specific target of audience. Facebook will also help you increase awareness of your brand and increase customer attribution as well as enable you to track results. The affordable costs of advertising and its proven effectiveness make it desirable for businesses that want to flourish. At the very end of it all, you will experience increase leads, sales, and revenue. To ensure that you hack this well, invest in a Facebook advertising specialist who knows the ropes of the trade.

CHAPTER 7: THE PSYCHOLOGY BEHIND FACEBOOK ADVERTISING AND ITS IMPACT

Do you ever find yourself checking your Facebook app a few times in a day? Mostly when you are idle? Facebook dominance, as a social media platform has created incredible curiosity for researchers worldwide. Over 90% of Facebook users admit to logging in the app several times throughout the day.

From a different perspective, some could term this as "being hooked." But what could make an adult "hooked" on a social media platform? Researchers have verified that there is a psychology behind the Facebook app itself that somewhat makes the users keep going back.

The psychology behind Facebook as an app is the same concept that makes Facebook ads very successful. From the extensive research done by various institutions and organizations, the psychology behind Facebook ads can be understood from comprehensive knowledge of the psychology of Facebook users.

No matter how introverted a Facebook user might be, statistic shows that one way or another, all Facebook users participate with their accounts. It could be actively or inactively. All the Facebook users fall in either one of the personalities below depending on the content they post.

The Agreeable

- These types of people tend to good at interpersonal relationships;
- They are, in all essence, more cooperative;
- They are helpful;
- They use Facebook to maintain honest interactions;
- Their interactions are with people they value;
- They do not speak ill of other people on the platform.

Conscientious

- These people have strong work ethics;
- They are highly organized;
- Their social responsibility is high;
- They are not frequent Facebook users;
- They post discrete and controversy-free content;
- They do not make harmful posts that hurt others online.

Extraverts

- They post frequently;
- They are generally positive people who use Facebook to communicate and socialize;
- The social network is often large;
- They are talking and upbeat;
- Of all five personalities, they post the most.

Overly Open People

- They share very frequently;
- They learn new information from the platform;

- They tend to explore new intellectual ideas on Facebook;
- They barely socialize casually.

The Neurotics

- They are generally negative people;
- They exhibit traits of low self-esteem, paranoia, bipolar among other traits;
- They post on private issues like their romantic relationships;
- Constantly seeking affirmation and attention through controversial posts;
- High chances of a neurotic going off on personal rants on Facebook;
- Most neurotics and anxious and highly sensitive people.

From the above characteristics, patterns of Facebook users are bound to emerge. For instance, agreeable individuals are more welcoming than Extraverts who tend to exhibit narcissistic tendencies and neurotics who are constantly seeking validation.

Another psychological mechanism that has a major impact on how people use Facebook is the psychological rewards from using Facebook.

The Psychological Rewards of Using Facebook and How They Impact Facebook Users

People are constantly going back on Facebook throughout the day because of the psychological rewards they receive from being on the platform. There is a sense of accomplishment that comes with using Facebook. Facebook has become somewhat an irresistible platform to many because of these rewards.

People are looking to either maintain concrete relationships on the social platform or get constant attention and validation. Whichever one it is, there is a mental satisfaction that every Facebook user gets.

Advertisers use the same psychology concepts to gain the most from Facebook advertising. The psychology behind Facebook advertising can be broken down into these single factors.

- The use of colors;
- The use of images;
- The use of compelling texts.

These are the key elements Facebook advertisers consider while putting up an ad on the platform. Apart from what people look at in an ad, advertisers also consider how an ad makes the people feel. They do this by selling the ideal picture of what people need.

With constant images of people doing great in their lives, there is social media pressure for people to keep up. People want to make their lives better. Most people who shop online are purchasing the experience rather than the products. Facebook ads capitalize on ideal selling. That is why the specifics of an ideal Facebook advertisement are centered on captivating texts, colors, and images.

The Psychology of Advertising Using Colors

Color psychology significantly increases the interactions by tapping into the most unconscious part of the human brain. Colors have a different impact on Facebook users. As an advertiser, understanding the basics of color psychology can be of great help. Details in the psychology of colors are utterly essential.

There are no best or preferred colors that are used to create enable quick psychological or emotional response. However, there are a few factors you can consider to increase traffic on your ads using colors.

- For instance, you can double a Facebook Ad CTR by including a colored border on your image;
- There are a few colors preferred by the female gender to other colors and vice versa;
- Conversion rates can be increased up to 60% by contrasting colors in two different links within one image;
- Conversion rates of your page can increase by 14.5 %when the CTA color button is changed from light green to yellow.

These are some of the small but significant aspects of color psychology.

Different Colors and How They Impact Your Facebook Ads

There are popular colors used by almost all the advertisers on Facebook ads. These colors represent different situations and convey specific messages depending on how they are used. Here are few of them and what they represent in advertising

Green

- Green, in most cases, signifies affirmation or positive action;
- It is associated with environmental themes;
- It is the easiest color that the brain processes;
- Green is at the top of the list for most popular colors with men;
- It is associated with shoppers who are on a budget;
- It can be used for social offers;
- Different types of greens are effective as color contrast;
- Greens are vibrant and at the same time mild to look at;
- The color green attracts the eye on an advert while at the same time, achieves certain emotions;
- You can say green is subtle and at the same time a vibrant color perfect for advertising.

Blue

- Blue is a multi-gender color perfect for advertising;
- It symbolizes security and trust;
- Darker blues signifies professionalism;
- Lighter shades of blue sooth the eyes and have a calming effect;
- On a Facebook Ad, blue can be used with another color contrast to avoid the Ad blending with the theme color of the app itself;
- It barely works for food items since people associate it with illnesses;
- It also depicts intelligence, logic, and competence;
- It can be used as a good primary color in a case where bold colors are included.

Purple

- Purple lies on the feminine side;
- It is also associated with wealth;
- According to statistics no men like the color purple;
- It is a great Facebook Ad color for a women audience;
- Purple makes a great color for ads that converse the message of wealth and abundance;
- It can be used on a demographic of senior women from the age of 60 years.

Black and White

- Black and white is safe colors;
- They both convey sophistication;
- They also signify power, intelligence, and sincerity;
- Black and white go together in most cases;
- The colors can be used to create professionalism in ads and bring out the sophistication;

Other happy colors like red, orange, and yellow are also used in the ads. They are intentionally used to attract the reader's attention.

The Psychology Behind Facebook Ads Using Texts

Specific words cause certain responses when used on Facebook Ads. For a successful Facebook Ad, well thought out texts are essential. Texts in Ads are used to bring out emotions or create psychological reactions.

Savvy Facebook advertisers take advantage of connotative words and phrases to achieve high responses. Connotative words and phrases have a much deeper meaning. Most effective words are short and precise but carry connotations. Here are some specific words that will make your Ad successful on Facebook.

Using "You"

"You" is a simple word, but when used appropriately, it can have such a major impact on Facebook users. The use of 'you' in an Ad commands attention. The word portrays that a product is built specifically for the person reading the advertisement.

- It can be used to compel your readers to purchase a product;
- It can be used to create curiosity of a product for a reader;
- Can be used to bring awareness to the specific reader about a product.

The Word "Save"

Who does not want to save some money or time? Facebook Ads are a perfect way to give discounts and offer coupons. Discounted products have better chances of penetrating the market and creating great profits. Using the word 'save' instantly grabs a lot of attention from Facebook users and will automatically create high conversions for you. A few examples of how to effectively uses the words 'save' are:

- "Save on eating out this holiday with these simple homemade food tips";
- "Increase your savings by up to 60% with these tips";
- "Save 40% buy making purchases in the next 12 hours".

Using the Word "New"

The word 'New' is crucial in advertising. With the production of new products every day, people are purchasing new. More people are moving away from the culture of minimalism and purchasing second-hand items to buying new and affordable items. A tip for bringing home when advertising the new products is advertising to the previous clients.

The Word "Proven"

The word proven in your Facebook Ad text conveys trust. It is an effective name on Facebook Ads as its meaning heavy. The valuation of a product can be recognized through the use of the word 'proven.'

You will largely increase conversions by the use of 'proven' as it portrays a guaranteed efficacy of a product or service.

The Word "Free"

The word 'free' has been proven to increase the efficiency of adverts by 30%. People all over the world, like products or services with free offers. You must, however, make sure you use the word free authentically with honest intentions to fulfill the free offer.

Offer free items or services and include them in the advertisement. For instance, you can offer free shipping to first time buyers of a product.

A text in your Ads brings out the intended emotions of a potential buyer and propels them to make a purchase. Conversations grow through how well your Ads capture the Facebook user's emotions.

Emotional language on the Ads brings out feelings and makes the Ad more effective. You can use emotional language to evoke fear, happiness, pity, humor, or encouragement. All these emotions will result in a reaction. Depending on how well you use the words, they can create amazing conversions for your business or product.

CHAPTER 8: HOW TO USE FACEBOOK ADS MANAGER AND SETTING UP ADS ACCOUNT

How to Use Facebook Ads Manager

Facebook continually introduce new features in the ad manager to make the campaign platform more intuitive. However, understanding how to use Facebook ads manager is one of the steps in creating a decent and more successful Facebook ad. Henceforth a successful implementation of a successful marketing strategy ensures that you reach more audiences while growing your brand and products.

As to create the most attractive and successful ad on Facebook and its subsidiaries, you need to understand how to get started with the Facebook business manager and the creation of an ad account. The two are the beginning of creating great ads while determining where and when to show to your target audiences. The chapter highlights step by step of how to use Facebook ads manager and the process of creating an ad account under Facebook business manager profile.

Guide on How to Use Facebook Ads Manager

Step 1: Create a Facebook Business Manager Account

After you decide that you want to advertise via Facebook ads, you are required to set up a business manager account and set your preferences about your brand and product. The ads manager is an essential tool as it provides you access to various areas such as your business pages and apps. Besides, it allows your team or other people to manage your accounts as well as optimize your ads and analyze performances.

As a beginner, personal Facebook account, business pages, and Facebook ads manager account possess significant differences, especially when it comes to business marketing strategies. Similarly, opening a business manager account and creating your advertising access also differ. Setting a Facebook ads manager includes providing your registration requirements, including your name, email address, and brand. When creating advertisements, the tool asks for details on your payments and billings, details about your product and company to display to the audience.

Step 2: Explore Your Facebook Ads Manager Account

Facebook ads manager comprises of all your needs in creating, editing, and making necessary changes to your advertisements. Facebook ads manager functionalities provide immediate impact to your ads, but Facebook enables you to set your parameters manually when you want. Some of the benefits of Facebook ad manager include the provision of management and modification of ads, monitoring of your existing campaigns, and setting of your target audiences.

After the creation of your business manager account, you may readily access the Facebook business manager dashboard after clicking a drop-down arrow on the right top corner of your page. The ads manager comprises of your account overview, campaigns, ad sets, and ads as well as other options including ad performance, breakdown, exports, filters, and charges on advertisements. You are then ready to set your standards and begin creating your marketing campaigns.

Step 3: Choose Your Objective

The Facebook business manager initially asks for users to set their objectives when considering utilizing Facebook ads when creating campaigns. Selecting the purpose of your ad is the first process of creating your advertisement by clicking on Create Ad at the top right corner. Facebook offers several categories of objectives to suit all e-commerce marketers via its platform. The types include:

- Awareness campaigns;

- Consideration campaigns;

- Conversion campaigns.

Under awareness campaigns, it involves reach and brand awareness, which creates knowledge and interest of your audience towards your products and brand. Consideration campaigns include traffic, engagement, app installs, video views, and lead generation, primarily attracting your audience to engage with your brand and products. Conversion, on the other hand, prompts your audience to purchase your products through product catalog sales, conversions, and store website visits.

Select the most convenient and sophisticated objective to meet your marketing goals, especially under the subcategories. Facebook will eventually create your ads through the set objectives after the successful creation of your campaign name. As such, you are ready to move to the next step as the advertisement is officially created. However, it is essential to select the most preferred option as it determines the performance of the following steps and the success of your campaign.

Step 4: Determine and Select Your Audience

Facebook comprises of over two billion active users who visit the platform daily, but they are not all your target population. As such, your target capabilities should solely focus on your audience, who are your potential clients. Facebook captures and records massive data about their users, including age, gender, location, education, interests, language, and behavior, among others. With such a large population, your target audiences are the crucial elements of your campaign.

Fortunately, the Facebook business manager offers the best filters to acquire your specific audience intended for your information. Some of the ways used to receive a new audience include lookalike, custom, and core audiences. Lookalike audiences are individuals generated from the existing audience as they possess similar features. Core audiences are obtained through setting your criteria manually and filtering the general population within Facebook. Custom audiences are created from your list of Facebook friends and contact lists as well as from former and current customers.

Lookalike feature of acquiring new audiences is one of the best as it primarily targets users with similar qualities to your existing audience. When creating a lookalike audience, you either choose your filters and criteria or select your preferences and Facebook create your audience automatically. More so, lookalike audiences play a significant role in expanding your market from your existing population to a broader range and equipped with similar features. According to Facebook, it is essential to upload a contact list of between one thousand and fifty thousand to guarantee the quality of your ads.

Step 5: Set Your Budget
Advertising in all platform charges a fee while growing your brand to reach a wider audience. The same applies to Facebook ads but provides different forms henceforth enabling users to take control of their budgets. If you have multiple active ads running, you can readily display each ad separately at alternating fees as you decide how much you spend on campaigns. Again, Facebook offers two methods of displaying your advertisements; daily and lifetime media spend, which also alter your charges.

Daily Media Spend

Daily media spend are regular fees charged from a given ad set at a default of $20.00, but you can readily adjust when the campaign is running. The charges may vary depending on how many times it displays on each audience or the platform in general. However, it is vital to spend as few fees as possible, for instance, $5 daily and make your ads run for about seven days continuously to enhance your performance. You may also decide to start with a $100 charge enabling the ads to display for at least two weeks for complete analysis for effective initial optimization and management.

Lifetime Media Spend

You may choose to display your ad for a longer duration charged somehow cheaper compared to daily fees. Lifetime media spend may range from a few weeks to months while considering aspects such as CPM and CPC. The two also affected regular media spend where CPM are costs charged per every one thousand impressions while CPC charged for every click on your ads. CPM is the most important when creating awareness of your brand and products. While CPC promotes your business as people click and visit your website or app and make a purchase.

Step 6: Choose Where to Display Your Ads

Since the acquisition of Instagram, Facebook has increased its advertising platforms hence enabling you to choose your desired areas to run your ads. Among them include mobile and desktop news feeds, Instagram, and Facebook messenger. Facebook ads manager offers several placements where you can select one or more categories where your ads will show and reach your audience.

Desktop and Mobile News Feeds

When you select your ads to show on news feeds of desktops, mobile, or both devices, they will run embedded in news feeds. It is, therefore, essential for brand and product awareness as well as engagement. When running ads with links or apps, ensure they are compatible with both or one device to avoid becoming annoying when clicked by your audience. The ads should remain responsive to both mobile and desktops, accompanied by a seamless experience.

Column Ad Displays

These are ads running on the right-hand column of Facebook and among the first designs of advertisement in e-commerce. The design is consistent with desktops users only and suitable for ads that promote your brand and products. Therefore, it prompts customers to purchase or click and learn more about what your business offers.

Facebook Network Audiences

Facebook has created multiple joint partnerships, and the same applies to create a network where your ads may show and attract new audiences. Some include mobile apps and websites henceforth maximizing exposure by displaying advertisements to viewers outside Facebook. Besides, Facebook networks enable ads to run in video views effectively while reaching people on other platforms, especially while browsing on websites.

Instagram

Instagram is another platform with millions of followers to different accounts, therefore, creating a favorable environment for ads. With Instagram being an asset to Facebook, you may choose to extend your ads to Instagram under all formats provided by Facebook. Like other platforms, Facebook enables you to expose your brand to Instagram to reach more audiences to come on board and purchase your products.

Step 7: Create Ads

After setting up your campaign, audience, and placement, now Facebook ads manager requires you to create your ad. First, you will select the mode of your creative display available in different formats, which include the carousel, single image, single video, slideshow, and collection. Each form accompanies varied ways on how your ad shows. For instance, carousel ads have scrollable images between two and ten, while collections comprise of both pictures and videos displayed on full screen.

After setting your format, choose your image, videos, or slides that stand out and focuses on your brand and product and grabs your target attention instantly. Check your thump stoppers by trying different images, slides, or videos to acquire the best ones. Upload the desirable one and populate and later make a preview to see your outcome. Other factors to watch out during ad creation include main ad text, headlines, and your brand link description. The main ad text has up to ninety characters, headlines not more than twenty-five while link descriptions should have a maximum of ninety characters.

Step 8: Add Your Campaign to Facebook

Once you have developed your ad accompanied with a call to action, sweet and straightforward thump, now it is time to click on Place Order option. Facebook will then screen your advert to ensure it complies with Facebook's Advertising Policies. If it meets, Facebook will approve, and your campaign will become live to your target population.

Step 9: Ad Monitoring

Another significant benefit provided by Facebook ads manager is the ability to monitor its performance, especially on the Return on Investment of your campaigns. During the monitoring process, the ads manager enables you to make changes where applicable while noting the performance on metrics. Clicks are one of the parameters to check to determine the number of times the ad has received clicks. Impressions are the number of times the ad has been viewed, and the conversion rate is the measure of the percentage of people who see, click, and make a purchase.

Facebook ads manager also enables you to set a reminder at specific times of the day where you will check and optimize your campaigns. As such, Facebook offers the best possible ways to ensure your receive customers despite the competitive marketing techniques in e-commerce. Tweaking the information provided including creative display, copy, your budget, and billing as well as your target population may alter performance. The technique is vital if you are receiving low traction on your ads.

How to Setup the Account

Creating a new Facebook ads manager account or claiming an already existing account provides a similar procedure for developing successful e-commerce marketing campaigns. Setting up an ad's manager account is conducted under Facebook business manager dialog essential for maximizing permission management of your brand.

Step 1: Create a Facebook Business Manager

Before setting up a Facebook ads manager account, you need to create a business manager profile found by clicking business.facebook.com and click Create Account. Enter the name of your business or brand, name, email address, and business page. In other fields below, add the necessary information correctly and submit your data to open Facebook business manager profile.

Step 2: Open Ad Account Setup Wizard

In the business manager profile, go to Business Manager Settings and click on Ad Account under People and Assets for already existing ads account. For newly created Facebook ads manager accounts, you will see a drop-down menu under People and Assets and select Add New Ad Account. Opening ad account setup for creating new accounts applies to both those with existing profiles or when new in the Facebook ads manager.

Step 3: Enter Your Details

Type your name to use in the ad account, choose your time zone, and the currency of your region, state, or country. Please ensure that the currency you submit is consistent with the coin you will use for your payments during the billing process of creating your advertisements. Facebook uses your time zone and currency to run your ads with an effort of displaying campaigns consistent with your region or country. Also, note that false information, especially on the money, may result in account closure. Add yourself as the account admin as well as your team participating in different roles in the ad account.

Step 4: Add Payment Methods

With all the above information provided, adding a payment method now activates your ad account. Select Payment Methods button and choose your preferred option and set it correctly for a successful account activation process. Once done, select billing country using either Credit or Debit Card with the previously indicated currency. Besides, ensure Credit or Debit Card information is consistent with your name as the admin as Facebook does not accept different titles of the same.

Step 5: Confirm and Submit Your Details

After placement of your information correctly, submit your data and your account will be activated almost instantly. Go back to the Ad Account option, and you will see Add New Account option indicating that you have an active account already existing. In your Facebook business manager, you may create a maximum of two ad accounts under as an admin as well as claim your account anytime in any profile.

Adding an Active Ad Account to Facebook Business Manager

Facebook Business Manager also helps when you have more ad accounts and wish to add them to your current profile. Readily select settings and click on Ad Account under People and Assets and select Claim an Ad Account. Provide your current ad account ID for campaign accounts or personal ID if using personal ad accounts. Claim the account and add it to your existing Facebook business manager and manage them with ease in one place.

How Technology Impacts Business Efficiency

To start and run a successful business without the input of technology these days is almost impossible. The possibilities of the business becoming a success are almost NIL. In a world that has nearly all the companies in various industries moving in the digital space, embracing technology is the only way to compete effectively. Many technology platforms are allowing business owners to gain maximum profits by integrating them into their businesses. From business websites to social media handles to applications meant for more natural service delivery, tech options are extensive.

The most modern technology is machine learning and artificial intelligence. It is completely changing the phase of many businesses and bringing about a revolution of efficiency and profit in minimal time. The TabSquare digital platform has embraced AI to fully maximize efficiency in its systems and service clients all around the world.

Tabsquare Machine Learning Proficiency in Running the Business

As a business operating with massive assistance of Tech, keeping up with the current tech trends is essential for the growth of the business. Consumers are the number one priority in any business. Ensuring their needs are met most professionally and effectively will undoubtedly result in a successful business. With the help of AI, TabSquare provides smart solutions that guarantee the profit and ensure quality and reliable customer service delivery.

The best part about the use of AI in TabSquare is the multilingual factor. A well-fed AI system can quickly detect thousands of languages across the globe. Limitations, in this case, become a thing of the past since business can reach out to a massive audience. The accuracy of AI in handling multiple languages is again a factor that screams efficiency in technology. With such a broad audience in business, the profits are bound to scale higher.

AI again wins in the world of advanced Tech since it enables businesses to take up data that is useful in future reference of the direction of the company. For instance, the broad information of the consumers fed in the AI system can detect future problems and trends. As a business, the ability to foresee an awaiting business calamity or progress can be extremely beneficial in future decision-making processes.

Time Saving Factor

The time-saving factor is the number one reason companies would consider while including artificial intelligence in their systems. The use of AI in TabSquare has substantially achieved this aspect. The system can provide fast and effective solutions that an average customer care agent would instead take time resolving. Also, it has been able to eliminate the inconvenience of a personal customer care agent when they have days off or when they have emergencies that prompt their unavailability. AI runs throughout the seasons and timings. It could serve your clients 24/7 as per your desired preference. The level of efficiency experienced in the time-saving factor of artificial intelligence system is worth investing in as a business.

Tech advancement creating efficiency in businesses is more than evident. The digital era is here and considering many enterprises are moving in the direction of technology and its advancements, entrepreneurs can only get excited about the possibilities of even better business operations. The success of any business in this new era solely relies on its technological versatility. More companies should embrace new technological advancements to make an impact in their space. Otherwise, they risk being thrown out of business by competitors who have already embraced technology and are willing to research more on the current business trends. Don't be left behind in this technological era.

CHAPTER 9: TYPES OF FACEBOOK ADS THAT YOU SHOULD AVOID

The Facebook business manager offers several types of ads essential for you while considering e-commerce marketing campaign. However, each type accompanies varying specifications, benefits, and detriments hence vital to select the ones desired for your campaign. As such, we are going to discover different types of Facebook ads you should avoid during the creation of your advertisement. The ad formats are from all Facebook audience networks, mobile and desktop, and Instagram platforms.

Dynamic Ads

One of the top Facebook ads types to avoid is the dynamic ad, which includes your audience viewing a similar production Facebook, previously saw on your website. Despite the product being more personalized and relevant to your target audience, the campaign displays the same information already perused by the user. On the other hand, if you decide to use dynamic ads to run your advertisement, Facebook enables you to save between thirty and fifty percent on costs for acquisition

Dynamic ads as well only apply on instances where you have more than ten images you wish to display in the form of carousels. However, they are only essential when in need of posting more than ten photos as carousels only allow a maximum of ten. Similarly, dynamic ads run at higher costs while solely providing similar outcomes compared to carousel ads type. Besides, dynamic ad displays are a modification of carousels with the ability to display more scrollable pictures.

Subsequently, when utilizing dynamic ads, they enable you to accomplish several e-commerce marketing objectives. Also, you readily select your desirable audience categorized as upselling and cross-sell products and viewed or added to cart but non-purchased audiences. This type of Facebook ads is among the best when it comes to the promotion of your brand and product by enticing your viewers to buy your goods or services. It, therefore, improves your campaign performance while delivering the intended information to your audience.

Features of Dynamic Ads

- Headlines have a maximum of 25 characters;

- The image size encompasses both 1200 x 628 and 600 x 600;

- The Ad text uses up to 90 characters while link description has 30 characters.

Canvas Ads

Canvas ads are another type that is interactive and engages your audiences about your content on Facebook. However, the canvas is only applicable and compatibles to mobile devices limiting desktop users to miss out on your ad. This type of Facebook ad may utilize any format of your campaign and people can swipe to view products. You can also tilt, zoom in and out to see the product or brand correctly as they load much faster compared to other types of ads. The ads display in full-screen mode, making users to readily watch, click, tap or swipe and engage with your brand.

As a type of Facebook ads to avoid, canvas advertisement hinders your access to the general audience found in the platform. This is because almost half of your target population may miss an opportunity to view your product or brand while using desktop devices, Facebook networks, or Instagram. Like most ad types, the primary function of Facebook as an e-commerce marketing platform is to reach more audiences henceforth maximizing your sales. With such presence of limits or restriction to mobile use only, then you are missing out on other clients fond of using desktops and Facebook web pages.

However, some of the benefits of using canvas ads include lifetime view of your products on mobile, delivery of complete immersive, and interactive campaigns online. This type also ensures that your audience readily accesses your business website or while viewing details within the mobile app. Canvas ads accompany different components and features which include;

- Headers with logos;

- Button to be redirected to offsite links;

- Autoplay options;

- Characters on headlines are 45 while ad copy text has up to 90;

- Text block;

- Image carousel.

Lead Ads

Lead ads are Facebook campaigns that focus on collecting user's email addresses for the benefit of creating mail lists to alert your audiences about your brand and products. The advertisement urges your prospects to sign up with your page enabling them to share or like your business. However, Facebook plays a significant role as it automatically populates fields where your prospects quickly sign up and grow your email list. Unfortunately, not all your target population would love the process of providing their details.

Your audience's data are then stored within your ads account and later moved to a CRM system which immediately automates the general process. Like other types of Facebook ads, lead campaigns also comprises of specifications which are paragraph format of context cards with headlines box up to 60 characters and Privacy Policy of website links, among others. New email addresses from prospects are added to a list already connected to service provider equipment with leveraged automated amenities.

Lead ads are important for advertisers who wish to create a long list of prospect's email addresses and set parameters on sending automatic them alert about new products, changes, or discounts. This type of Facebook ads is, therefore, not recommended for beginners interested in creating awareness while promoting their products and businesses. More so, lead ads are most suitable for established brands who wish to expand their market. Besides, it enables their prospects to remain updated on the trending products through newsletters or occasional notifications.

Page Post Text Ads

Page post text ads are among the ones you should highly avoid as they have limited evidence about your product or brand. This type primarily engages your audience with plan texts posted on your Facebook business page but likely to deliver poor outcomes. Page post text ads typically show on right columns of your feeds on both mobile and desktop devices. Plan texts possess numerous disadvantages compared to its benefits. Some of the negatives are poor attention generated from prospects; it lacks eye-catching features to attract your audience and limited room to monitor and optimize its performance.

 On the other hand, page post text ads have benefit, for instance, direct interactions with your audience despite deteriorating your engagement practices. However, direct contact has a limited area to click, scroll, or even tap to view the products being advertised. That said, ensure you avoid using this type of Facebook ads to as it is among the classes with the low-performance outcome despite being the cheapest method of Facebook advertisement. Page post text ads may even become one of the worst choices for you, especially when they lack boosted page posts from Facebook.

Single Image Ads

Single image ads are among the most common today and involve quality photos displayed on both Facebook and Instagram. The images are of 1200 x 628 pixels, therefore, enabling you to run quality photos in marketing your products. However, single product pictures may seem bias and sometimes overlaid with multiple texts. Despite being among the most used formats today, it is important to utilize other types to show your prospects more about your business and in detail through various images.

Ads containing single images are suitable for displaying funny or happy people or customers as well as beneficial ones such as when offering discounts. However, you may choose other options for new businesses to showcase several elements of your business. For instance, newly established enterprises require descriptions of the brand and products as well as some information about your company. As such, one image ad becomes a challenge to highlight all the information. Beginners should henceforth avoid single image ads while creating Facebook ads to run.

Page Likes Ads

Page likes ads are campaigns to grow likes within your business page with an effort to reach more prospects and build a broader fan base. A page like ad is essential, especially when you need your fans to view any notification about your brand or product. Facebook enables you to reach between two and three percent of your audience with an immediate call to action button after your placement. Facebook also provides you with an opportunity to set your parameters on whom to attract to become your fan. That is, you can choose your target audience from the filters and advertise the message to the desired individuals.

However, page like ads has minimal impact during the creation of campaigns to enhance awareness and product promotion. For beginners, the development of advertisements with excellent features accompanied by well-detailed descriptions encourages your audience to purchase your products. With Facebook settings, the low audience reaches while using a page like ads, seek other types of ad formats to reach a broader target population, and create a more considerable margin of prospects. Subsequently, page like ads may attract unintended individuals; therefore, may involve people not interested in your brand or products.

Abandoned Carts Ads

Abandoned cart ads are another Facebook format campaigns which are necessary, but you should avoid during the creation of your e-commerce marketing strategies. In a study conducted by the *Baymard Institute,* about seventy percent of all shoppers globally abandon their carts while shopping in different firms. As such, abandoned cart ads tend to let these shoppers back to the store and continue shopping or complete their purchase. Facebook launched an abandoned cart ad with personalized features crucial for targeting these individuals.

You may use funny videos or well-illustrated images to make them go back to their carts and complete the purchase. Nevertheless, such ads tend to contain low engagement and seductive nature suing the individual to really continue shopping. More so, the shoppers may view the ads and ignore while others may not abandon their carts but have an intention of keeping with shopping later. We would, therefore, recommend that you avoid this type of ads as they have minimal impact on driving shoppers back to your store when they abandon or halt their shipping.

Facebook Messenger Ads

Facebook messenger ads primarily focus on targeting Facebook messenger mobile application for those who like chatting with friends. The ads run in the main tab enabling a user to view it while in the messenger inbox between different conversations. If interested, the user may click on the ad, and it may redirect to either your brand's website or view the products. The ads can only be considered neither by those using their inboxes or asset during campaign creation.

Features of Facebook Ads

- Maximum image size is 1200 x 628;

- Image ratio 1:9:1;

- Characters include 30 for the description, 125 for the text and 25 for the headline;

- Minimum width of images 254 x 133.

Viewing the ads in the conversation is an excellent option for you, but more prospects may not use Facebook messenger frequently hence limiting your audiences. Similarly, the platform may show a limited number of ads compared to the main page or other platforms vital for your campaign. As such, Facebook messenger ads format should be avoided. That is because you may choose to run your ads in the news feeds or Facebook audience network and reach a broader audience. It, therefore, increases your advertising performance while increasing your fan base as well as your prospects.

Choosing the Best Facebook Ads Format

Facebook's tens of Facebook ad formats may create a challenge, especially for beginners in determining which to use when creating their e-commerce marketing campaigns. Deciding which form to use may primarily depend on the stage of your products or brand, nature, and objectives. When in need of creating awareness, then the ads should solely deliver the message intended. Beginners may end up selecting formats resulting in lower performances, therefore, leading to failure in Facebook ads marketing.

Similarly, different types of Facebook ads remain introduced to achieve a particular objective, as such, always check on your goals before deciding on your factorable format. The real purpose, audience, and formant go hand in hand in the creation of the most successful Facebook ad essential for your campaign. Before selecting your desirable format, understand the different types of Facebook ads. Learning about these formats ensures that you can readily optimize and make necessary changes in the right form collected.

CHAPTER 10: FACEBOOK PIXEL AND BUSINESS AD MANAGER

A Facebook business manager is made to help users, and business owners manage and organize their businesses.

For users to create a Facebook ad with the business manager, they must first create a Business Manager account. This is a simple process that has clear guidelines. However, you should first create a Facebook profile. Facebook allows a maximum of two business accounts; you cannot have more than one business manager account.

Here are the steps you should follow when creating a business manager account;

1. Ensure that you have a personal Facebook account which helps in identifying the user;

2. Link the account to the website of Facebook, i.e., business.facebook.com;

3. Click on the create account icon;

4. Write a unique business name to avoid conflicts and confusion with similar businesses. You should conduct a name search with a professional before settling on the final business name. This is also the right time to attach your work email as well as any other important address

details. Where you will also have to select its primary page and enter your name and work email.

Once users are done with setting the business manager account, they can now send invitation links to their friends. To reach a wider audience, you can start the advertising campaign.

Adding an ad account in the business manager account is very easy. Here are a few steps that you should follow for better results:

Step 1. On your business manager's home page

Click on the add ad account button. Once you have clicked it, you will have two options of either adding an existing ad account or creating a new ad account.

It is important to note that if you are creating a new ad account, you should use the name of the business when asked to name the new account. When done with the process, you will then click create an ad account. This step gives users the ability to have a brief idea of how their ads will look like.

Step 2. Installing a Facebook pixel

For a user to be able to set up an advert on Facebook, he or she needs to install the Facebook pixel on their website. It comes with greater benefits and attracts more potential customers to business websites.

But what does it entail? A Facebook pixel is a tracking code that enables Facebook to identify people who visit their customer's website. It creates a customized audience and creates ads for a potential market. It can also help businesses to identify potential and future customers based on the data that they collect from those who visit their website.

Step 3. Setting up the target audience

After installation of the Facebook pixel for the ads, you should now set up the target audience. This involves selecting the audience that you would like to reach out using the ad. It enables business owners to get optimum results from the ad that they have shared with the audience. It also ensures proper usage of resources for the user will not use excess budget while the product is reaching the wrong audience.

In choosing the right audience, factors such as age, gender, location, and demographics should be put into consideration. To access the audience tool, the user should log in the business manager account under assets and select the audience option. The audience can be categorized into; lookalike audience, saved audience, or custom audience.

The customize audience is that audience that is already familiar with the user's product and engage now and again with the user through Facebook page and website.

The saved audience, on the other hand, is the audience that shares a common interest with your line of product. The saved audience is a good start for a first-time marketer who is advertising his or her product to a new market.

A lookalike audience is that which resembles the same interest as those of the customize audience that the user has already interacted with.

Step 4 Creating your ad.

After you are done with all the above steps, you will be in a good position to create the ad and run it through the business manager account via the Facebook page. Before running the ad though, the user must most importantly not forget to categorize his or her ad campaign into three levels i.e., the objectives, conversions, and sales or clicks. With all these in mind, the user or the marketer will be ready to run a very successful ad campaign that will yield optimum results.

In conclusion, we do realize that the most important thing even as a user runs an ad through the business manager is always to have his or her objective set right. In everything that a person does even in our normal day to day life, objectives are what always guide us to success. For example, when a marketer wants to advertise the product, he/she should be well aware of the benefits that will accrue from that campaign. When advertising a product, the user should always make sure that he considers the interest, age, gender, location of his or her target market before running an ad on Facebook via the business manager account. A marketer must also have a reasonable budget so as not to be constrained so much when running an ad campaign.

Facebook is a global platform that is used nearly by every person in the world, has proven to be a great place where many businesses have managed to grow through advertisements. This is because business owners can target the right market and audience in line with the products that they are dealing with.

How to Use the Facebook Pixel?

Facebook pixel is an analytical tool that is used to find out the performance of a user's advertisement. It enables business owners to understand the actions that visitors take when they visit their website. Every time potential customers visit their preferred website through a Facebook ad, Facebook pixel analyzes, measures, and reports the action. This will help business owners to know the type of actions visitors perform when they visit their site. It, in turn, helps in creating a customized audience or a target market. Through Facebook pixel, the social media giant can know people who are most likely to take similar actions if they visit your site and can help set for a user lookalike audience. Some of the actions that Facebook pixels perform include the collection of information and data that will help a user in tracking conversion from Facebook ads and building a target audience to be used in the future.

The use of Facebook pixel for marketing is very important for it plays a crucial role in providing information that a marketer can use to help in creating an ad that will have an optimum return. The information gathered can also help the user to get the right target audience for his or her ad. This informs the business owners on who is most likely to take any action, for example, purchasing a product after seeing the advertisement. As a result, this would eventually increase the rate of conversion from a Facebook ad.

How Facebook pixel can help you with marketing

1. It helps you know how many visitors visit your website after seeing the ad on Facebook. It also helps in tracking your visitors and enables you to see which device they mostly use to visit your website. For instance, you can check if most are using their mobile devices or their personal computers.

2. After visiting your website, the Facebook pixel can help you retarget your audience. It allows you to see the type of product a visitor was interested in. For instance, a customer can select a product on your website and leave it in the chart without finalizing the transaction. With Facebook pixel, you can be able to re-advertise the product to the specific client as a way of enticing the client.

3. Facebook pixel also allows a user to create a lookalike audience. Besides, its groups those who already visited the user's website and those who might tend to have the same interest as those who already visited the site. It will consider the interest, location, gender age, and demographics of the look-alike target group.

4. Facebook pixel also helps business owners to optimize the conversion rate of their Facebook ad. With the data gathered the user can focus his or her ad to a specific audience which will, in turn, enhance the conversion rate to the maximum. It does this by increasing the possibility of the audience visiting the website and taking various activities such as purchasing a product.

5. As visitors visit your website and do purchases, the Facebook pixel can help the user to group his audience according to the value of the product they purchase or which they are interested in. For example, it can help a user to know the audience that is most likely to purchase a product of high value and those that are interested in products of low value. This will help the user to group his or her audience per their level of income.

Facebook Pixel Standard Events

Events are actions that always take place when people visit your site through Facebook ads.

Facebook has 17 Facebook pixel standard events;

1. **Purchase -** this is when a visitor visits your site and completes a purchase and makes the required payments for the product.

2. **Contact -** this is when the targeted customers visit your website and make a telephone call, sends SMS or email to

contact your business regarding a specific product or service.

3. **Donate** - this when a visitor in your website donates to your organization or event that had been advertised on Facebook

4. **Customize product** - this is when a customer picks a specific product, e.g., a product of a specific color or size.

5. **Schedule** - this is when a customer books or schedules for an appointment with your business.

6. **Find a location** - when a customer searches for the physical location of your business.

7. **View content** - when a customer lands on a specific page or category of the products on your website.

8. **Subscribe** - when a customer pays a subscription fee for a product or service on your website.

9. **Add to chart** - when a customer adds a product that they are interested in their shopping cart on your website.

10. **Add payment information** - a customer adds his or her payment information during the purchasing process on your website.

11. **Lead** - a customer signs up for a product trial in your website or identifies themselves as leads in your website

12. **Complete registration** - when a customer completes registration form or subscription form on your website

13. **Search** - when a customer uses the search engine in your website to search for a product or service.

14. **Initiate check out** - when a customer starts the checkout process after buying a product on your website.

15. **Start trial** - this is when a customer signs up for a free trial of a product or service on your website.

16. **Apply** - when a customer applies for a product or service in your website

17. **Add to Wishlist** - when a customer adds a to a Wishlist on your website.

Here is the step by step procedure of creating Facebook pixel in the Facebook manager account;

Step 1. Visit your business manager business account. On the top of the business manager, the home page, click on the menu at the top (it has three lines) then select create pixel from the asset column.

Step 2. Click create pixel to begin the process.

Step 3. Select your business name

Step 4. Select the + add button

Step 5. Insert the name for your pixel

Step 6. Enter your optional website URL

Step 7. Select create

The final step is installing Facebook pixel on the user's website. Here the user must choose the option he or she is going to use to install the pixel. There are three options that a user can choose to install the pixel. One can either copy-paste the pixel code manually or if he or she is using a third party, then the user may use a tag manager plugin to install the pixel. The other option is emailing the pixel code developer or a trusted friend who can help with the installation process.

If the user decides to use the copy and paste option, he or she will see the install pixel base code page. He or she should click on the code box to copy the code in the clipboard. After this, all the user has to do is to paste it in the header tags of their website under the SEO (Search engine Optimization) settings. If a user is using a third-party service, he or she should just do it the same way in the header tags of his or her page.

Next, the user should be free to install the Facebook pixel code. The user should then click next to get a snippet of code they install on specific web pages to be able to track actions taken on those pages.

The final step in the installation process is testing the pixel status. To do this, the user should go to the Facebook business manager account and select pixels. If the pixel status is active, it means the Facebook pixel was installed correctly. It may take between 20-30 minutes before the status of the pixel is updated.

In conclusion, Facebook pixel's main objective is to help a business or a marketer to get to know more about the people who are always engaging with its(business) content. A user can use this valuable information to create content and product that has a better appeal to the target audience.

CHAPTER 11: ADVERT MISTAKES THAT FACEBOOK MARKETERS SHOULD AVOID

Facebook ads are one of the best tools to use for both new and existing businesses. However, for the ads to give satisfactory conversion, every marketer needs to select the best ad type for their trade wisely. To decide which the best type of ad to use is, some things should not be overlooked. The business owner should first consider setting up the goals they intend to achieve as the beginning stage of ads creation. These goals should be tangible so that they will assess and know when they need to change their ad type. There are four primary goals for every business. These are;

- Creating their brand awareness;

- Generating leads to their products;

- Customer care;

- Converting traffic to sales.

These are general goals basically for most businesses. However, every business should set their own more specific goals and decide on how to meet them. Once the goals are set, the next step will be to understand the different types of Ads available. With different types of ads for different marketing goals, your specific goal will help you decide which one of them is best for your business. You will then customize the ad type you choose to use and create it in a way to suit your business. When the time to assess progress comes, you will know if the add was helpful. If you don't meet your goals, you will know what did not work and try a more suitable ad type. Experimenting with different types of ads will give you lots of information regarding what works for you to meet which goal.

In this chapter, we shall look at some types of ads that should be avoided at all cost by any Facebook marketer.

Page-Like Ads

These are Ads that focus on increasing the number of likes on your page. Having high traffic on your page could increase your sales. It's good to note, however, that it's not guaranteed that everybody who likes your page likes your products. Such ads will rise the likes on your page drastically, but in most cases, the conversions will not pace up. This is because someone may have liked the page without necessarily even looking at what is displayed on it. Instead of targeting likes that might not give your business, it will, therefore, be better to have a few likes from people who genuinely like your products. Others, like the engagement ads, would instead help you gain likes, comments, and shares on your post. This is likely to give awareness and at the same time, convert traffics to result in sales.

Facebook Stories Ads

These are ads that will appear for 24 hours and then disappear. If you want them to appear longer, you should make sure to save them. People who may miss Facebook for a period of more than 24 hours may not see the ad because it will have disappeared when they go through their app account. More so, Facebook stories ads alone will not effectively work alone.

Untargeted Ads

General ads that do not target a particular group of people may end up as a waste of time and money. This is because people who will not get interested in your products will be seeing your ad and may not respond to it. For example, if an untargeted ad is able to reach one thousand people, half of them may not get interested. Targeted ads do better because they seem to appear to a specific group of people. The groups are defined either in a specified age group, a particular region or with a specific shared interest. Targeting ensures that 100 % of the people who see it will in one way or another connect with the ad.

Pop Up Ads

These have proved to be the most annoying type of ads among most Facebook users. Mobile surveys have also seen most people disliking and disapproving them. If people do not like these types of ads, chances are they will not even click on them to know what they are advertising. Bad enough, most people will block them from appearing. It's good, therefore, to use Ads in a way that will not annoy people to avoid giving people a negative attitude towards the product. Instead of getting interested in knowing more about the product or your business at large, potential buyers may get irritated by the site of any advert from your store.

Ads with No Set Goals and Objectives

The first step in the creation of an advert is supposed to be the setting of goals to be achieved. The goals help you with determining what kind of advert you need to create. Some Facebook marketers encounter difficulties making any positive progress because of not setting their objectives. This occasionally leads to losses that could not have been encountered if they had a clear intention before setting the advert. Having set goals also enables you to assess the progress of your business. It also helps you understand how each type of advert has assisted you in meeting the marketing funnel stages' goals. With no goals, Some Facebook marketers choose wrong adverts for their products. This, at times, confuses the minds of their audience since they find the advert irrelevant. Consequently, part of the audience will drift away from the product.

Ads That Target the Wrong Objective

Some Facebook marketers want to sell as soon as they post their first Ad. This does not catch the audience that just found out that you exist. Like every other engagement, it's wise to consider giving before asking to receive. It is always good to consider the marketing funnel stages and create ads considering the different kinds of people likely to view it. For an extremely new seller, it will make more sense if they create an ad that gives awareness before they start their sale. Once you have an already engaged audience selling to them will be easy altogether. At the same time, having more people recognize your brand and liking your page and website should be the first thing in your mind. Once you have more followers, you can then try converting the viewers to buyers. Most marketers rush into conversion ads while they have no audience to convert. This mistake makes the advert to end up making zero achievements.

Lack of Using Facebook Pixels for The Ads

Pixels are important units to all Facebook marketers for them to build a custom audience. Facebook pixels optimize adverts for conversions and also track conversions on every Facebook marketer's website. However, some Facebook marketers tend to ignore this vital unit. As a result, they miss getting views from their viewers. Clients' opinions are an essential aspect of the growth of any business. They help every business owner to assess and understand how people feel about their products and the business as a whole. This will help them decide on changes they need to make either in their targeting or their ads type. They will also understand the market trends as potential buyers tend to compare you with your competitors. Evidently, anyone who does not use Facebook pixels will be missing a lot.

Adverts with Irrelevant Headlines

Most people either don't like reading a lot of content or are lazy when it comes to reading. Long complicated headlines in an advert will most probably put off such people since they will view it as a boring post. Some other headlines are too wordy that even some Facebook users who may want to read may not understand what is being advertised. The many words make the advert seem irrelevant to people who view it, and it may cause a lack of interest to Facebook users. When people lose interest in the advert, most definitely they will not take time to think about the product leave alone considering buying it. The business will most probably not achieve its main goal as per the advert and may also incur losses since the ads could be paid advertisements.

Advertising Multi-Products at One Time

Many Facebook marketers tend to advertise many of their products at the same time. When such adverts may give excellent results, they require a lot of consideration on how they are set. When put in slides or videos with clear descriptions on each slide, they can be the best kind of ads for awareness. However, the marketer must have the best of professionalism to create beautiful and organized ads. Photos are not ideal for such adverts unless put in a slide. People will not scroll down on a post whose first photo is not of something they are interested in, which leaves some products unnoticed. Some marketers also market with so many products in the same post, giving links that direct viewers to the website. When traffic moves to the site, it can be overwhelming, and some inquiries may not be well responded to, which can put off impatient buyers. Such adverts are also time-consuming since it takes time to refresh your creativity. In the long run, some products may lack your attention on your website such that even clients may notice you are inconsistence. Inconsistence is very dangerous as it can lead to people doubting your credibility, which can cause a downfall in the business.

Poorly Targeted Ads

Some marketers tend to focus on a small number of audience or a very large number. While targeting a large number can increase their sales, it's not guaranteed. A large number can cause too much congestion on your website with ninety percent of your audience's not interested in your product. Some marketers target a very small group which is not healthy for the business. For you to increase sales, you need to have a high number of people who are viewing it. However, the target population must be the relevant people who need the product, and in a locality that you can efficiently deliver. For example, if a seller is marketing cartoon themed school bags, it will be useless to target youths aged 12 – 20 years. As much as they are very many on Facebook, the cartoon-themed bags may not make sense to them. If the same person targeted young parents aged 20- 35 years, they would most likely have convertible traffic on their website. If they targeted the population of 12 – 35 years male population, they also might have so much useless traffic on their wall. The cartoon-themed school bags will catch the attention of people shopping for kindergarten and primary children. Most shoppers will be women and not men.

Ads That Concentrate on One Form of Advertising

Many Facebook marketers focus too much on one type of advertising. While the video form of advertisement can be catching, it may not be suitable for every Facebook user. Videos may be discouraging to some people who may not have time to watch but prefer short descriptions. Other people go through Facebook when they are in the office working or waiting to be served. Watching videos in such a place may cause disturbances, and so they pass the advert without opening to see what it is about. In such a case, a written advert featuring pictures of the product will be the best to catch such an audience. Some people also tend to think that videos are edited to create an impression to the viewer and hence ignore video adverts. It's important for everybody to concentrate on different forms of advertising to attract more of the audience who have different preferences and advertisement beliefs.

Monotonous Adverts

Your audience gets used to your ad in a few days or weeks. It's advisable therefore to keep refreshing them with new ads so that they will not get used to one and get bored. Even though you do not have different products every few weeks, there are still things you can do to show changes in your advert. This means you have to be creative every time you make an ad, or else people will start ignoring them. You can refresh your adverts by

- Turning statements in the previous ads to question forms;
- Change the personification;
- Edit images to change some features like filters, edit texts, add or remove logos, use gifs instead of photos;
- Change background colors;
- Increase or decrease words in the description.

Through the edits, it will make the audience want to see what you have for them every time they see your adverts. It keeps them wanting to see more of what you have, and this helps keep your audience engaged.

Unproductive Paid Ads

While paid Ads are more productive, they are also the riskiest type of ad that any Facebook marketer should be careful when using. This is because the ads require one to invest real money for you to run your advertisement. Facebook paid ads can lead to a significant loss to the marketer if he or she does not have a clear guideline on how it should be created. They are one reason why many Facebook marketers tend to make loses other than the expected profit. When you realize your ad did not deliver per your expectations, it's wise to consider revisiting it before investing more on the same. Try to check where you went wrong and make the necessary changes before giving it a second shot. When paying for your ads, it's also good to consider a reasonable budget. A meager budget can allow your competitors to outdo you while a very high budget can increase your losses. When your advert starts performing well, you can gradually begin increasing the budget. If you realize that your paid ad is performing poorly, it's wise to stop running it and work on improving it. By doing this, you will be controlling your chances of incurring heavy losses. When running paid ads, it's advisable to be diligent so that you don't pause or stop ads before your target population gets to see them.

BONUS: SPLIT TESTING AS A WAY TO MAXIMIZE YOUR IMPACT

As promised, I wanted to offer you a special ***bonus*** chapter that would help you do even better at creating strong performing advertisements. This special bonus chapter discusses split testing and the power of split testing as a way to maximize your impact and increase the value you gain from your advertising budget.

What is Split Testing?

Split testing ads essentially means that you run two or more advertisements, each of which are slightly different, to see which ones perform the best. When you use split testing properly, it allows you to accumulate a large amount of information about your audience in a relatively short period of time. Through that, you are able to begin understanding your audience in a deeper manner which means that future ads are more likely to convert with great success *and* you know what types of products or services to offer your customers to boost sales. While this particular method for getting to know your audience will cost money, it tends to be faster and far more accurate than nearly any other method out there.

Facebook itself has a split testing feature built in, which is also known as A/B testing. This feature enables you to make your two separate advertisements and run them, and it will use Facebook's built in analytic trackers to ensure that you are getting the results you desire from your advertisements. Plus, it will allow you to compare the productivity of both of the ads to see how well they performed.

What Should You Split Test?

Split testing can be done on any number of things in your Facebook advertisements. When it is being down, however, it is more useful to do it on smaller differences rather than larger differences so that you know exactly what your audience is and is not responding to. For example, you could split test with things like:

- Colors of the call to action button;
- Images vs. videos;
- Words in copy;
- Specific call to actions ("Sign Up!" vs. "Learn More!");
- Audience targeting;
- Element positioning;
- Landing page design.

By split testing with these subtle differences in your advertisements you can get specific information regarding what works best and what doesn't. This way, you can begin to construct advertisements that reflect the findings of your A/B split test practices.

The key to making sure that your split testing practice works is to create two advertisements that are almost identical, except for subtle differences. If you attempt to try too many different aspects all at once you will find that you struggle to identify what was working and what wasn't. As a result, you may not be able to duplicate your success because you have not gotten a clear understanding as to what it was that your audience really wanted.

How Much Of Your Budget Should You Place Into Split Testing?

At first, your entire budget should be placed into split testing so that you can start to get more specific findings on your audience. You should take your entire budget, set the goal for how many different advertisements you are going to try, and then allot your budget accordingly. This way, you have enough money to run each of your split tests.

If you are new to Facebook advertisements, you should try running each split test for at least five days before cancelling it to see your results. If your results seem highly obvious much sooner than that, though, then you can take action accordingly.

If you were to try one split test at a time, for five days, then this would get you 12 advertisements per month. This means that if you had a budget for $1000 for advertising, then you should allot about $83.33 per advertisement so that you can begin to see what your results are like.

If you are not new to Facebook advertising and you already get generally decent results from your advertisements, then ideally you should only use split testing when you are unsure about what will work. If you find that your current ads are not getting you the results you desire and you want to try expanding into making more money through Facebook advertisements, then at this point you might want to start allotting some of your budget to split testing. In this case, you should keep at least 50% of your budget for your ads that are already working, even if they are not working exactly how you wish, and use the other 50% of your budget to conduct split testing. This way, you can see what is likely to work and you can start improving the quality of your standing ads according to your findings, without excessively dirsupting your existing results with your advertisements.

What Should You Do When The Results Start Coming Back?

As you begin running your split tests, you will find that in some cases the advertisements receive fairly similar results whereas in other cases the results are completely different. How you manage your advertisements will ultimately depend on your findings in this case.

If you find that your advertisements are performing fairly similarly, you should let them run all the way through the entire five days, or whatever allotted time period you have provided them with. This way, you can get conclusive findings from your results. If the results are incredibly close, you may want to make a few more tweaks to the split test before running it again to get a more conclusive finding. Or, in some cases, you may find that people do not particularly care more or less in one way or the other for the shift that you are making.

If you find that one ad clearly outperforms the other ad to the point where one is barely performing at all, you should pause and cancel the advertisement that is not performing well. Rather than spending money waiting to see if it does better, you can invest that money into prolonging an advertisement that is already working well, instead. This way, your budget is spent wisely *and* you learn about your audience through the power of split testing.

Refrain From Overtesting Your Audience

As helpful as split testing can be, it is important that you do not over test your audience as this can lead to wasted money, confusion around your brand, and poor results from your ad budget. Ideally, split testing should be used sparingly to ensure that you are still creating consistency in how you show up and that you are able to turn great results from your advertisements.

As well, make sure that you avoid hyper-segmentation, which ultimately means that you run a split tests where you are getting far too specific on who you are advertising to. If you find yourself getting too specific, you are going to end up wasting money because you will not turn any results from your audience.

When you run split tests, make sure that you have an audience of about 500,000+ people to advertise to, depending on your budget and who your actual target audience is, so that there are plenty of people to collect numbers from. This way, your budget will still turn you back with some results from your tests that will enable you to make greater success with your Facebook advertisements overall.

Conclusion

Facebook adverts are with no doubt the best tools for any marketer to reach their audience on Facebook. However, wrongly chosen ads can lead to losses for the same business. Worse still, the right ads done incorrectly can lead to the downfall of any business. Therefore, wisdom dictates that every marketer should first understand their product well enough to know which population to target. Once they have understood the product, the marketers should then set adverts for their products, following the advert funnel tips to ensure the audience is covered at all levels. The adverts should be created considering already set strategic goals. Once the adverts are posted to run on Facebook, it's the job of the marketer to follow up and see how they are doing, as they make necessary adjustments. Finally, when the marketer is sure they have the best ad for their product, it's time to run them on Facebook. They should be sure to set their budget reasonably and maximize their potential to maximize their profits.

Made in the USA
Middletown, DE
29 December 2019